Video Ministry

Using Media in Worship without Going Hollywood

Constance E. Stella

Abingdon Press
Nashville

Video Ministry: Using Media in Worship without Going Hollywood
Copyright © 2006 Abingdon Press
All rights reserved.

This book is printed on recycled, acid-free paper.

Library of Congress Cataloging-in-Publication Data
Stella, Constance E.
  Video ministry : using media in worship without going Hollywood /
    Constance E. Stella.
    p. cm.
  ISBN 0-687-49345-5
  1. Public worship—Audio-visual aids. I. Title.
  BV288.S74 2006
  246'.7—dc22

                                                        2006005225

06 07 08 09 10 11 12 13 14 15—10 09 08 07 06 05 04 03 02 01

MANUFACTURED IN THE UNITED STATES OF AMERICA

For Reid,
my partner in all things, whom I love

Contents

Foreword

Old men often are tempted to look back and reflect on the past. One explanation for this behavior is that our past, as measured in years, is ten to twenty times the size of our future. By contrast, both the nine-year-old and the teenager assume their future will be several times the size of their past. They do what I do. We use as our key reference point what we have in abundance.

For example, during the first twenty-three years of the twentieth century the Consumer Price Index doubled from 25 in 1900 (1967=100) to 51 in 1923. That brought it back up to the same level of 51 that it had been in 1800! It doubled again between 1923 and 1968 to 105, doubled again between 1968 and 1979, doubled again between 1979 and 1993, and will probably double again between the time a baby born in 1993 graduates from college. People from my generation not only remember when a three-cent postage stamp cost three cents, but also remember that was all it cost to mail a first-class, one-ounce letter!

My early experiences in life plus my study of American history in high school taught me to expect a period of inflation should be followed by a period of deflation. That deflationary era followed the close of the War of 1812, the end of the Civil War, and the peace treaty that ended World War I. The discontinuity came when the 1950s brought a period of inflation, not deflation. That was followed by inflationary periods in the 1960s, the 1970s, the 1980s, the 1990s, and the early years of the twenty-first century.

Another example of how discontinuity has dominated the economy and the culture of the past half century in the United States is a central theme of this book. This has been the discontinuity in communication. I was born into and grew up in a culture in which I was taught that the most effective channels of communication were touch, facial expressions, the spoken word, body language, the printed word (for me that came early in life since I was the youngest person in a family that included three older readers), music, laughter, applause, printed pictures, and photographs.

At about age nine or ten I was introduced to that new channel of communication of projected visual imagery we called "the movies." It was not, however, described as a channel of communication. Motion pictures, except for the newsreels, were almost universally identified as entertainment. One consequence today is that the use of projected visual imagery in proclaiming the gospel of Jesus Christ may evoke among mature adults a response that ranges from "distracting" to "entertainment" to "blasphemy."

When I turned nineteen, I enlisted in the United States Army Air Force. There I first discovered music as a truly powerful channel of communication. World War II taught me that music and projected visual imagery are the two most powerful channels of communication if the goal is to rally people in support of a cause called patriotism.

Several years later my wife, Agnes, and I agreed that one of the most valuable legacies we could bequeath to our children would be a love for the printed word. Therefore, after our first child was born we agreed we would not purchase a television set until after our youngest child had learned to read and to enjoy the satisfactions that came from reading. As the years rolled by and the babies continued to arrive, we stuck firmly to that principle. If our family political system had been a participatory democracy, we would have been outvoted in a 3-to-2 referendum by the late 1950s. We stuck to our convictions and wrote off that discontent as the price that had to be paid for adherence to principle. Eventually we became a family consisting of two parents and four deprived children.

At this point it is not irrelevant to note that many decades later the oldest of those four children is a professor of philosophy, an extreme illustration of dependence on the printed word and the spoken word for the transmission of abstract concepts. The second is a retired publisher who chose early retirement to move to Thailand in order to publish books in Laotian indigenous to the culture of Laos for deprived children in that world economy. The third grew up to be a teacher and recently evolved into a librarian. The fourth is a transportation consultant who depends heavily on both the spoken and the written word for the communication of ideas.

The big point of discontinuity in our family history came in 1964 when baby number six arrived. Shortly after that surprise our second son, at age twelve, delivered what he had identified as a dismal trend. "You have told us we can't have television until after the youngest child learns to enjoy reading. That means, if you two keep bringing babies home from the hospital, I'll be through high school and will have left home before we get TV!"

One consequence was that a year later we purchased our first television set. A second consequence is our second daughter, born in 1961, has organized her adult life around creating visual expressions of art, not the printed word. A third consequence is our youngest son and his wife, an art teacher, organized their own business designed to create and maintain interactive educational websites for museums. In other words, in choosing a vocation the four oldest of our children, who were reared in a learn-to-read-and-enjoy-reading-pre-television home chose vocations organized around the printed word. The two youngest, who were reared in a home with television, make a living in vocations organized around visual imagery.

From a larger perspective one consequence of this discontinuity with the 1950s, represented by projected visual imagery moving ahead of the printed word as a channel of communication, is how Americans keep up with the daily news. Television has moved ahead of newspapers in the delivery of the news. Most Americans, especially American men, spend more hours per week watching television than they spend reading books.

For many pastors the most threatening consequence of this discontinuity in communication can be summarized under the word "choices." Where can the Christian believer in America go to receive relevant and inspiring messages about Jesus Christ? In nineteenth-century America the most common answer was as far as you can walk in an hour or as far as your horse will take you. For most Americans the range of choices was a single-digit number. By the 1930s radio had expanded that to a dozen or so choices. By the 1960s the combination of the privately owned motor vehicle and television had increased that number to several dozen. Twenty-first-century technology, including the iPod, already has increased that range of easily available and very low cost choices of excellent preaching to hundreds and soon to thousands.

In addition to expanding the number and variety of choices, this expression of discontinuity has raised the bar. In the 1950s a reasonable estimate was that in terms of both content and delivery the active preachers in American Protestantism could be divided into three categories. One-third were above average to excellent. Another one-third earned a grade of average, and one-third were below average. The parish pastors who were below the median often could "get by" if they excelled in pastoral care or competence as leaders or teachers or with their skills in interpersonal relationships. One extreme example of this last option was the congregation averaging three-hundred and fifty at worship and at least three-hundred of them modestly identified themselves as "one of our Pastor's five or six closest personal friends."

Today, if they so choose, four out of five of all adults in America have relatively easy access to watching and listening to someone proclaiming the gospel of Jesus Christ who clearly ranks, in terms of content, delivery, and personality, among the top 3 percent of preachers in American Christianity. The bar has been raised on what is required to be ranked as a great motor vehicle, or great hospital, a great shortstop in major league baseball, a great college or university teacher, a great surgeon, a great single-family home, a great President of the United States, a great elementary school, or a great preacher.

Concurrently the demand for high-quality, relevant, and challenging preaching designed to help people move to the next stage of their personal spiritual journey as Christians is at an all-time high. One alternative for small to midsize congregations is to seek a pastor who excels in interpersonal relationships and pastoral care. Another alternative is to supplement the ministry of that loving shepherd or excellent leader by outsourcing the preaching and relying on videotape or a DVD for the delivery of the message on fifty weekends out of every year.

Another consequence raises the question: What did you buy when you purchased this book? For those of us reared in the pre-television culture the answer is obvious. "I bought the book and the publisher threw in the DVD." The buyer born after 1960 is more likely to reply, "I bought the book because I wanted to share the DVD with people in my church."

The contents of this book are based on several assumptions, most of which are spelled out in the text, but eight merit a brief mention here, partly because they will help define contemporary reality and partly because all eight are threatening to those who hope this book will help them perpetuate "the good old days."

The first, which may be the most threatening, is that Americans born and reared in a culture dominated by projected visual imagery probably will outlive those of us born and reared in the pre-television era of the 1940s and earlier.

A second assumption is that projected visual imagery and music now rank up there with touch, facial expressions, and body language as the five most powerful channels of communication. This is most obvious among people born after 1980. Some would add the cell phone and the spoken word to that collection, but the rapid evolution of the technology of the cell phone suggests that visual imagery continues to be more powerful than the wireless transmission of the spoken word.

Third, the pace of change has been accelerating at an unbelievable pace! The obsolescence of film and the acceptance of the digital camera represent one current example. A second example is the cell phone. A third is the reliance on projected visual imagery in creating multi-site congregations with one name, one message, one staff, one governing board, one budget, one treasury, and a dozen or more weekend experiences at several locations.

Fourth, in those congregations in which women formerly constituted 55 percent to 70 percent of the adult constituents, the two most productive roads to increasing male participation have been (a) challenging and equipping male-dominated teams of lay volunteers to be engaged in doing ministry and (b) a greater reliance on projected visual imagery in telling the story of how God gave his only son for the salvation of sinful human beings.

Fifth, the use of both music and projected visual imagery are not only compatible with the corporate worship of God, both can be useful in achieving the goal of creating a participatory style, as contrasted with the 1950s presentation format, for the corporate worship of God.

Sixth, and perhaps this should be described as a consequence, not as an assumption, the larger the size of the congregation in American Protestantism and/or the faster the rate of numerical growth and/or the younger the median age of the constituents, the larger the proportion of paid staff who are lay specialists, often part-time, and the smaller the proportion who are ordained generalists.

Seventh, and most important, this book, as well as the ministries of the Church of the Resurrection, affirm the role and the potential impact of the gathered worshiping community. It can be more influential in this century than ever before in the history of Christianity! That is the number-one reason for my commending this book to you. It really is a book about initiating planned change from within an organizational structure. This is a book about how to do ministry in twenty-first-century America.

Finally, and the second-most-important assumption, the channels of communication for telling the story of Christ's impact on our world must be consistent with and supportive of the definition of that congregation's purpose and its reason for existing in the twenty-first century. That is the place for your congregation to begin planning for its role in the third millennium.

LYLE E. SCHALLER
Naperville, Illinois
February 8, 2006

Acknowledgements

Many people have influenced this book—far too many for me to name here. But I want to attempt to capture the importance of their impact, so I'll try to identify them at least by group. I would like to thank:

Stu Fedt, whose patient explanations from the early years of Saving Grace Productions helped me understand how things worked, and who designed our first incredibly flexible technical systems, literally transforming dream into reality.

The wonderful people who joined our staff in those first few years. In particular, Glenn Whitney, Anne Martin, Paul Borchardt, and Patti Hirst, who helped build this ministry, and taught me much that I hope will be useful to others through this book.

The volunteers whom I've been privileged to serve alongside. I appreciate their willingness to learn and to take risks in ministry. There are too many leaders to name individually, but these committed servants have pioneered new territory in the operation of technical ministries, which has already influenced many churches. The fellowship and joy shared with these friends and co-laborers is sustenance for me.

The Church of the Resurrection. It's been a rich and rewarding experience to serve on this staff. I am grateful to the church for the allowance of time to work on this project. And I'm daily in awe of my colleagues there, whose influence is evident in each chapter of this book.

The Saving Grace Productions staff at the time of this writing—Taski Arenas, Frank Gentile, Brent Handy, Stacey Hughes, Nick Kastelan, Roberio Moreira, Dave Pullin, Kristin Thompson, and Stephanie Smith—who demonstrate daily what it means to serve on purpose, and from whom I have learned so much. It's hard to imagine a more devoted, talented, intelligent, and hilarious group of people to spend each day with.

A handful of other people who should be mentioned by name, because this book would be substantially different without them. Sue Thompson, for her friendship and rock-steady commitment. Sandy Thailing, for his willingness to try something new professionally, and for helping to create the Resurrection style. Craig Janssen for his encouragement and mind-opening perspective. Marty O'Connor for his annual sandy-footed guidance and pep talks. Rev. Lucinda Holmes for her understanding of human motivation and for urging me to try to understand people first. Kristin Thompson for proving that students can teach more than they learn and that teachers can learn more than they teach. Michael Sipes for his incredible mentoring at times that made the critical difference, for being my cheerleader, and for understanding the guy on the back row. Frank Gentile for his enduring partnership, for reminding me to see people's hearts, and for getting it done and making it fun. Steve Eginoire for showing me the value of 85 percent, and for sharing his gift of clarity.

The Holy Spirit, whose guidance had a lot to do with this project, too. During times when I hit a wall and didn't know how to get past it, I felt the Holy Spirit move in and take over. I am so grateful for that presence in my life!

Rev. Adam Hamilton. It's impossible for me to describe his influence on this book. It literally would not have been possible without him. He is responsible for nudging and pulling me into ministry and has influenced virtually everything I've done professionally since that time. The ideas in this book are mostly things I've learned from Adam, repackaged in a new context. I count it as a life-changing privilege to serve under his leadership.

The members of my small group, my beloved companions in Christ.

My parents, Jeanne and Jerry Epple, who provided care for my family and me so often during this process.

Sam, Olivia, and Francesca: Thank you for enduring all things. I cherish you.

Introduction

This book is intended to encourage and offer real help to the thousands of people who serve God in local churches, creating video, graphics and other media for worship. It is written from a particular perspective and is aimed primarily at ministry leaders who share that perspective. This book is written mainly for the mainline.

As I understand it, the term *mainline church* was coined late in the nineteenth century and referred to the row of Protestant churches which formed a neatly dotted line down Main Street in Philadelphia. Over the years, as with all language, interpretations and connotations of the term *mainline* have changed. For some, it may hold a negative connotation. For me and for the church I serve, mainline is a term associated with the strength and integrity of our denominational traditions.

In fact, part of my hope in writing this book is to advance in some way the renewal of the mainline church. Our Lutheran, Presbyterian, Episcopal, Methodist, and other churches have been in a now boringly famous decline. But these denominations serve Christ and welcome Christ's people in ways no other type of church can. It is imperative that the decline be stopped and that the Church be revitalized.

To revitalize is to give new life. Media in worship is part of the new life of many churches, and it's reasonable to think that the trend will continue. Media has been important in my own church, the United Methodist Church of the Resurrection, in suburban Kansas City. My pastor and boss, Rev. Adam Hamilton, says that media in worship has been "invaluable" and has helped him to be a more effective preacher. Our church holds as a key value the renewal of mainline churches, and I believe that media in worship must be part of that renewal.

Church of the Resurrection has grown quickly. We are led by a pastor who is gifted with deep and wide vision. Adam sees things no one else sees, far off in the unimaginable distance. And his view includes people and ideas that are typically in tension with one another. This wide-angle lens somehow results in a uniquely focused picture of reality.

Our church now sits firmly planted in the extreme center, the very middle, the *via media*. We aim to hold in balance evangelism, social holiness, biblical integrity, thinking-persons' questions, the gospel of grace, and the concept of personal holiness. The nuance and context of this balancing act is tricky to communicate. There's a lot of gray in this picture—not so much black and white. Media has been a critical part of sharing that picture in our church. Our congregation and our community know who we are and what we're about in large part because of our use of media.

Do you know what your church is about—who you are as a congregation? That's the first, and perhaps most important question addressed in this book. Resurrection's success has been partly due to the strong sense of purpose we've had from the beginning. Purpose is the first of six principles that I believe form the foundation of an effective media ministry. The others are values, culture, vision, excellence, and meaning. This book is based on these principles.

I have met and talked with pastors, volunteers, and staff in churches all over the country who are frustrated in their attempts to build a media ministry. Often, it seems to me, they have begun building without first laying the foundation. Some churches start doing media because it seems to be expected, the thing to do now. Often it's an attempt to draw a younger crowd. Or the new pastor is enamored with PowerPoint®. Or a member just made a donation and wants it to go to a projection system. These may all provide valid impetus for starting media ministry, but if I could urge churches to do one thing, it would be to back up. Before you go further, make sure you've laid a strong foundation. My prayer is that that this book will provide you with some of the tools, the courage, and the motivation to do just that.

Saving Grace Productions is the name of Resurrection's media ministry. The ministry has gone from one part-time staff to ten staff and nearly two hundred volunteers in eight years. It has been an awesome journey. We've made lots of mistakes, some of which I share here, hoping you might avoid them.

In case you wonder about the name: In 1997, we began seriously talking about starting a media ministry at Resurrection. Our church's new sanctuary was under construction and would require image magnification because of the room size (1,500 seats). As I considered a leadership position in this new venture, I wobbled back and forth between wanting to do it and not wanting to do it. In my prayerful search for discernment, I was reading through Ephesians and came to chapter 2, verses 8–10. *"For it is by grace you have been saved, through faith—and this is not from yourselves, it is the gift of God—not by works, so that no one can boast. For we are God's handiwork, created in Christ Jesus to do good works, which God prepared in advance for us to do."* I knew that ego and product-centeredness would be a problem for me personally and that it could become a problem for the ministry.

The Ephesians passage seemed to acknowledge that challenge, but it also revealed the answer. In those words, I felt God telling me, "This is what I want you to do, and I will show you how to do it." Saving Grace Productions was born.

About the Way the Book is Written:

This is not intended to be a scholarly work. I read and studied dozens of books and essays, and I've interviewed several people in preparation for this book. But you will not find quotes, statistics, or research findings here. It is not a technical or "how to" manual; the bookshelves are crammed with those already, and technology has never been my focus. (I'm thrilled by what media can do, but I'm only marginally interested in how it works.) Neither is the book intended to be a spiritually deep work. My faith informs everything I do, I hope, and discipleship is a critical part of what we should do in *every* ministry, including media ministry. I hope there is a measure of inspiration and spiritual nurturing for the reader in these pages, but that is not the main objective.

In the end, I felt that personal experience, real-life illustrations, and techniques that have been tested in the local mainline church would be the things most useful and encouraging to the reader. I've tried to write the book I wish had been available to me when I began working in ministry in 1998. So what you'll find here is a mostly personal story. I hope you find in it a renewed sense of excitement for your ministry, an understanding of the foundational principles for starting or growing your ministry, and the encouragement to apply both.

CHAPTER ONE

Purpose

The tall and lanky man walked through the doorway, nodding politely to the elderly woman who handed him a bulletin. His well-dressed wife walked ahead of him, eagerly. "I hope I can spot one of our neighbors or someone else we know," she thought. "That'll make him feel better about this."

At the same moment, he said to himself, "I hope nobody we know is here. Then we'll have to talk, and this will just last longer." She scanned the crowd for familiar faces. He quickly slipped into an empty row of seats. It was the last row, farthest from the chancel, closest to the door. She slid into the seat next to him, trying not to reveal her irritation. "Those clouds better not mess up his game this morning, or it'll be another three months before we go to a church again," she silently fumed, fixing her gaze on the window.

He noticed the gray gathering, too. "All I wanted to do this weekend is play one round! If I don't get to the golf course today, I'm going to blow a gasket. I should have been out there an hour ago, instead of sitting here wasting time. This'll be just like all the other ones, a bunch of crap."

The guy on the back row. He is a figurative person, and a real one. Figurative because he represents all the people we aim to reach each weekend in worship. Real because he is a real person with a name. Actually, he's a composite graph of many people. Men and women of varied ages and backgrounds. Accountants and business executives and doctors and computer programmers and homemakers and journalists and salespeople and insurance agents and lawyers and carpenters and electricians. People who begrudgingly come to church, ready to dismiss it, looking for a bone to pick. People who sit where no one will see them and where their escape is quick and sure: on the back row.

The purpose of our congregation is to create a community where non- and nominally-religious people are becoming deeply committed Christians.

The purpose of our church dictates the purpose of our ministry. In my own church, we are to use technical arts, video, and media to create a community where non- and nominally religious people are becoming deeply committed Christians. Here's how we talk about it on the media ministry team: "We're creating a welcoming place where the guy on the back row will meet and fall in love with Jesus Christ, so that he walks out as a new man."

It's a beautiful irony that nearly all the volunteers and staff on our media team were people on the back row at one time. Today, if you were to wander into our control room or skybox or audio booth and ask the people there to explain their purpose, they would all (I hope!) recite our church's purpose. And they would tell you about the men and women on the "back row" and how everything we do—the way we shoot, the director's cues, the graphic design, the way we videotape interviews, the lighting design—is aimed at them.

In this chapter, we'll examine the principle of purpose. We'll start with a brief discussion of church purpose. Then, you'll see how we apply the principle of purpose in our work within a video-based media ministry, with specific examples on the DVD accompanying this book. Next, you'll learn how to apply the principle of purpose in the way you form and operate your media ministry. Finally, you'll review a list of pointed questions. It's my hope that these will become a resource for you and that over the years they'll help you apply the principle of purpose in your ministry.

Remember the back-row people. We'll return to them again.

Forming Your Ministry on Purpose

Many are the plans in a human heart, but it is the LORD's purpose that prevails. (Proverbs 19:21)

Church of the Resurrection's purpose statement is the basis for everything we've done as a church since our inception in 1990. Prospective new members learn it before they join the church. Adam Hamilton preaches on it specifically once each year, and incorporates it into sermons throughout the year, reminding us of it regularly. Kids in Sunday school learn about it. Teens in the youth group recite it. Rooting everything in our church's purpose has probably been the most important influence on our video ministry, Saving Grace Productions. But that importance goes far beyond the ability of our people to spew out the statement word-for-word. You see the most meaningful impact when you look inside the ministries, when you look at the work that's done in service of Christ, and when you look at how that work is done. Here, you see new ministries growing out of our purpose and you see our purpose fulfilled in ways large and small, year after year.

Rick Warren wrote in 1995, "Nothing discourages a church more than not knowing why it exists. On the other hand, the quickest way to reinvigorate a plateaued or declining church is to reclaim God's purpose for it and help the members understand the great tasks the church has been given by Christ." In *The Purpose Driven Church*, Warren lays out a thorough and compelling argument for the purpose as the critical foundation for every church. Warren makes it clear that we must start here, no matter the age or size or type of church we serve in.

I am frequently surprised when I talk with staff, pastors, and laity in churches with purpose statements that are so broad or vague that they are impractical. Or, worse, they have no purpose statement at all. This begs the question: If you don't have a purpose statement, do you really have a purpose? Some may say, "A statement is just words." "Too constricting." "Our purpose as the church is biblical and universal; it needs no statement of explanation." However, a purpose statement defines what your church is about and, by inference, what it is not. Your purpose statement differentiates your church from other churches. "As I prepared to start Saddleback Church, one of the most important factors I discovered in my research was that growing, healthy churches have a clear-cut identity," writes Warren. "They understand their reason for being; they are precise in their purpose. They know exactly what God has called them to do. They know what their business is, and they know what is none of their business!"

Nondenominational, nonconnectional, and nontraditional churches are springing up in nearly every city, and many are growing fast. These churches are influenced by many movements: Willow Creek, Saddleback, Vineyard, Calvary Chapel, multi-site, and more. These churches present the gospel in a form that is accessible, un-mysterious, understandable, compelling. Their worship can seem like an extension of our contemporary society and culture, not very churchy at all. We should be grateful for and encouraging of our brothers and sisters who are giving birth to new movements of God's inbreaking Spirit; they are bringing people to Christ, which is what we're all expected to do! But one sort of purpose is not effective for all congregations. One language of worship can't be authentic expression for all people. For so many, the "anti" or "non" type of congregation just doesn't feel right. A sense of being rooted in the ancient, of being connected to others through tradition, the richness of liturgy and creed—these are authentic for many of us. And these expressions can still pull people into a faithful commitment to our community.

We in the mainline[1] congregations are formed in a different way, and we are uniquely capable of serving God's purpose in that way. During the big boom of growing nondenominational churches in the last two decades, we have been rather quiet. Our mainline systems continue chugging along, but ever more slowly. There's the opportunity! After decades of decline, we can gather up the things that make us strong, we can observe what's worked—and what hasn't—among new expressions of God's Spirit, and we can earnestly seek God's will for our congregations. We can acknowledge the void that exists in many of our congregations and redefine ourselves, starting with our purpose.

The Purpose of Our Church Is...

(1) **Evaluate Your Church's Purpose.** In evaluating your church's purpose, try to discern what God expects to happen in your area. What are the unmet needs your church could be meeting? Then, review your church's resources and strengths. Where do the needs and resources overlap? God may lead you to a clear purpose, showing you how your church is uniquely suited to meet a need in your community. Lovett Weems asks church leaders "What is the one thing that, if I don't do it, no one else is likely to be able or willing to do, but which simply must be done."[2]

(2) **Communicate Your Church's Purpose.** Write your purpose out everywhere, teach it to everyone, and use it as the measure for success and as the marching orders in every ministry in your church. And carefully reevaluate it—ideally every other year.

(3) **Write Your Church's Purpose.** If your church has no specific, clear, written purpose statement, write one. It should say what

---

[1] For a definition of "mainline," please see the Introduction.

[2] See Lovett Weems, *Church Leadership*, 2nd edition (Nashville: Abingdon Press, 1993).

exactly you'll do, for exactly whom, and to what end. "Spread the Good News to All!" is admirable but functionally useless. Spread it in what form? By what means? To whom? Where? What will you expect of them when you've spread it? What will you do together because of it? Implicitly or explicitly, your purpose statement should answer these questions. Your media ministry must begin with purpose. And its purpose must grow out of the church's purpose. That's why this is so important.

> Your media ministry must begin with purpose. And its purpose must grow out of the church's purpose.

Sometimes a media ministry team is unable to influence or clarify the specific purpose of an entire congregation. This sort of clarifying strategy is usually accomplished among the leadership or board. If you find that such matters are very difficult to influence, keep trying with diplomacy, asking the questions and pressing for clarity. Meanwhile, focus on the purpose of your media team, even if it's in the vacuum of a fuzzy-purposed church.

Now let's examine how the principle of purpose influences the actual work of media ministry.

Applying Purpose in Your Ministry's Work

What does the principle of purpose mean in the work you produce? How does purpose affect the way you do what you do?

Purpose should inform and shape everything you do, from web pages to bulletin covers to projected lyrics to video production. Start by considering your "target audience." Your purpose is aimed at somebody. Who? The unchurched in your area? College-age people? Your city's homeless men and women? An aging, rural population?

Next, figure out how to communicate most effectively to that audience. How do they typically get information? TV, newspaper, neighbors, the web? What's their communication style? Linear, text-based, fast-paced, open-ended, mood-based, environment-driven? An upper-middle-class, well-educated congregation is likely to respond to a cognitive, text-driven, classic, clean, linear approach. A working-class congregation might expect more edginess, more graphic arts, a more in-your-face style. A college-age group could be drawn to a non-linear, free-flowing, pared-down, experimental media style, with fewer effects and less text. For this congregation, media may be used not so much to present factual information, but to create an environment.

The work you produce should match your audience. This may seem like an esoteric exercise, but if your media doesn't feel right, it won't work. A pattern is repeated in lots of churches: No one takes the time to think about the impact of purpose on the work. And soon the congregation simply rejects media in worship altogether.

Following is a sampling of ways to apply purpose to media in several church scenarios, including real-life examples from Church of the Resurrection. This is by no means an exhaustive list, just some ideas to get you thinking.

- **In a church where the purpose is to provide engaging worship**

  Use thoughtfully selected photos or video clips as backgrounds for lyrics, to pull people into the expression of worship. If the song praises God's creative power, use scenes of natural wonders. For a prayer-song, use scenes of candlelight, with slow dissolves between stills or slowed-down video. For a song of gratitude for salvation, put together a sequence of images of the cross. You get the idea.

- **In a church where the purpose centers on teaching**

  Create an assortment of images to reinforce the teaching points. With your "audience" in mind, use graphic images, text, photos, maps, charts, illustrations, original art, and web screen shots. The sermon is the obvious place for these, but experiment with using images at the welcome, during transitions to prayer, as part of the liturgy, and during music. At each point, consider what you're hoping to teach the congregation, and imagine ways to underscore that teaching with media.

- **In a church where the purpose involves missions and social holiness**

  Illustrate the critical needs that your church is focusing on. Keep those in front of the congregation, with photos or video or articles in the newsletter or on the web. Also illustrate the ways your congregants can serve; and use media to make it easy, with bulletin tear-offs and web-based registration. Don't forget to show the congregation the impact it's making, in very specific ways. Use photos or video to introduce the people whose lives are impacted by your church's ministry. And regularly reflect back to the congregation the ways *they* have been changed by their service, too.

- **In a church with a purpose focused on building community**

  Reflect your version of community. Charge folks with the task of shooting pictures or video at every major church event. Regularly share the photos or video clips with the congregation. Piggyback on the photos or videos, and use them as an opportunity to invite others to participate. "You've seen how much fun the Ice Cream Social was…We hope you'll join us next week for the Harvest Festival!"

- **In a church where the purpose is to prepare the congregation to evangelize**

  Combine the ideas for teaching and missions. Consider providing teaching-type tools on the web as a resource for your members.

- **In a church where the purpose is to reach the unchurched**

  Use video to appeal directly to non- and nominally-religious people. Address their questions head-on. Confront their misconceptions. Give them information. All of this should be wrapped in humility and grace. Use testimonials to allow people to ask their questions openly and honestly. This validates the question and honors the person asking it. You'll also find people in the congregation who have moved from skepticism to belief. Let them share their stories, too. Ask them to share the ways they were transformed, and to share what that felt like. This provides a great modeling opportunity for the unchurched people in your pews.

Show your congregation examples of what it looks like to live as a Christian. Work this into every video or graphics or other media project you can. Show the nuts and bolts, the everyday decisions, the struggles and rewards of a life with Christ. Again, you'll coax along the cynics with this strategy.

Use real people in photos and videos. Use people from your congregation who live where you live. Avoid stock photos of people; they look like what they are: models posing in New York or Los Angeles. Most non-religious people have already been turned off or turned away from church, and anything that smacks of phoniness will provide another example of how Christianity is full of fakes.

Applying Purpose in the Formation and Operation of Your Ministry

What does this principle of purpose mean to *the formation and operation* of media ministry? At its most basic level, purpose means your media ministry functions to serve your church with strength and vitality, like a strong arm on the (church) body.

Lots of times—more than I'd like to admit—my media ministry team has not felt like a ministry functioning with "strength and vitality." Obstacles rise up unexpectedly. Plans give way to chaos. Opposition's foothold becomes a stronghold. However, we have learned:

1. How to see above and beyond the obstacles rising in front of us, to keep our eyes on and follow God's will for our ministry.

2. How to stay flexible and cheerful when everything we've planned seems to topple over, as if blasted by a gust of wind. And that planning is critical on three levels. It protects the work that is most critical (purposeful). It reduces the frequency and velocity of the "gusts" and increases our ability to respond effectively to last-minute changes.

3. How to manage the inevitable opposition to ministry. To remember that it's a largely unavoidable, maybe even natural part of the ministry. That sometimes opposition is a result of our own mistakes and is God's gift of instruction for us. And that sometimes opposition seems strongest when our ministry is approaching something big—as if Satan is setting snares in our path to keep us from reaching our goal.

Purpose in the Formation and Operation of Media Ministry
(1) Seek God's will, above and beyond and around obstacles.
(2) Diligently plan, to do God's will.
(3) Abide in God's grace, for yourself and for others.

Your ministry's purpose is the one critical thing that God needs your ministry to do. Your ministry's purpose must grow out of and help to fulfill the purpose of your church. Your ministry's purpose is its reason for being. It answers the question, "Why are you here?" Obstacles, chaos, and opposition can deny your ministry the power to work on purpose. Let's examine each.

Obstacles

"Problems are really just opportunities for growth!"

I hear the positive biz-speak lingo for problems or obstacles and, depending upon my mood, I either chuckle or cringe. Yep, the bad stuff that happens in ministry is usually a great chance to learn something, even if it's just, "I'll never do *that* again!" Most of the time, though, I seem to experience the junk as hardship more than anything. I find too often that I'm stuck in the nitty-gritty, down-and-dirty details of the latest trial. I see everything that's wrong, and as I concentrate my gaze, the wrong seems to grow. I think they call it tunnel vision. Can you imagine being deep inside a dark and narrow tunnel, feeling like you're able to tilt your head back, stretch out your arms, smile, and breathe in deeply, ready to embrace this "opportunity for growth"? It doesn't happen that way for me. When I'm in the tunnel, I am anxious and defensive, and I whimper. Not exactly open, let alone strong or vital. But I do know the one thing that shatters the tunnel, and you know it too.

Rejoice in the Lord always! (Philippians 4:4)

Remember to remind yourself,

I can do all this through him who gives me strength.
(Philippians 4:13)

The leader of any media ministry must cultivate the ability to see above and beyond and around obstacles, to see something different. This doesn't mean the obstacle is no longer there, or that you should necessarily ignore it. But an obstacle really can lead to opportunity, if we can keep from getting stuck staring at the obstacle. If we try to see beyond it, we often find an entirely new way of seeing. A new idea takes shape. A different approach becomes clear. And the coolest thing is that this new way of seeing has consequences beyond the original obstacle. Often, these new ideas and approaches lead to new ways to grow the ministry, to provide better support for its staff and volunteers, to do better work. In other words, seeing beyond the obstacle can help our ministries function on purpose.

Seeing Above/Beyond/Around Staffing Obstacles

Your ministry changes a lot, right? And sometimes staff or volunteers don't want to change along with it. At a certain point, those folks can become obstacles—for the ministry's work, for the team's morale, and for you as the leader of change. Other volunteers and staff sometimes suffer from a different challenge: They get bored. These folks join the team and soak everything up, learning fast, cross-training. They hit a plateau, and begin to disengage. Sound familiar?

This scenario has played out several times on ministry teams. We've found two strategies to mitigate this risk. First, create a narrowly defined and finite job description for the change-resistant person. The duties should be finely focused, with strict parameters. The tasks may be a "step down" in responsibility and authority. Don't characterize it as a demotion. Rather, it's a position that allows the person to remain in his or her comfort zone, allowing the rest of the team to move forward unhindered. At the same time, when you sense that people are becoming disengaged, find them a new challenge. What's something that you've wanted to do, but can't get done? Can this person take on the task? What skills does the person possess, and how might those be employed in new ways to grow or improve the ministry? Prayerfully compose a list of options, and discuss them with the person. Chances are, he or she will be surprised and delighted by your confidence, and will take on a new challenge for you.

With staff and volunteers, we must look at the whole picture. Where are the gaps, redundancies, weak points, and bottlenecks in our work? Where are the strongest places? Would change there help or hurt? Would this area be even stronger if we bolstered it somehow, or is it better left as it is? Who has potential to learn new skills or to move into leadership? Look at your volunteers and staff as a puzzle. If you need to shift one piece, it might be God's good timing for you to shift others, too. Use this sort of planning to make multiple changes at once. It may seem like your puzzle needs shifting almost constantly. If so, you're not alone. Within our media ministry, we do this sort of people/task shuffling every eight to twelve months.

In 1967, NASA astronauts Guss Grissom, Ed White, and Roger Chaffee died in a fire inside the Apollo I space capsule as it sat on the platform at Cape Kennedy during a routine test. America's space program, then barely beyond its infancy, might have been shut down in short order. Understandably, a maelstrom of investigations, questions, and accusations swirled around NASA and its private-sector suppliers. The culmination came on Capitol Hill, at heated congressional hearings. Frank Borman, another NASA astronaut, testified at the hearings. His most compelling testimony to the House and Senate committees regarding the cause of the incredibly tragic deaths of his friends had nothing to do with scientific failure, mathematical miscalculations, or mechanical design flaws. As he explained it, NASA built the Apollo module to work in space. They were testing it to make sure it worked properly in space. But the tests were being conducted on the ground, and it never occurred to anyone that this particular problem might be possible. The team was keenly focused on testing for space flight, and failed to consider how the spacecraft materials might react differently on the ground. In his testimony, Colonel Borman pressed the same point over and over: "I did not consider it as hazardous. I do not believe that anyone within the test organization or the program office considered it hazardous. And this is the unfortunate trap through which we fell…We did not consider this problem sufficiently…We overlooked the potential hazard…We overlooked the possibility." What caused that horrible accident? Lack of imagination.

When we're confronting obstacles, it's easy to get stuck gazing at only one part of the problem, to get tunnel vision, and to miss the forest for the trees. We, all of us, too often suffer from a lack of imagination.

Here's the thing you already know: There's only one reliable route to the kind of imagination that leads us above, beyond, and around obstacles: communion with God through prayer, study, meditation, worship. This communion comes through our openness to the Holy Spirit prompting us directly, and through others. It may be virtually impossible for you to worship regularly in your church. If so, what gets you in a place where you can really spend time with God? Solitary prayer in your home? Some sort of regular chapel gathering of your worship team or staff? The accountability and open discussion of your small group? A walk alone in the woods? You need to determine where and how you can most freely speak to and listen to God. And you must carve out the time for it regularly. When you face a really impressive obstacle in your ministry, get yourself to a place of communion with God for at least a couple of hours. Open your heart and mind. Take a few deep breaths, and see how far you can see. Obstacles get in the way of purpose. But God, your creator, who provides you with all that you need, equips you for ministry, and gives that ministry its very purpose will give you imagination to see above, beyond, and around. We can never really do it alone.

The Flexible Optimist

One of the ways God prepared me for ministry, I believe, is by making me a flexible optimist. Others might call it "unrealistic" or "ambitious." Media ministry, maybe because it is still new and not universally accepted, can be even more challenging than other ministries in the congregation. Compounding this is the fact that the media ministry leader is often the only one who understands the ministry and its unique challenges. You're a lone ranger! If you're a flexible, adaptable, easygoing, happy, optimistic person, you'll roll with the changes and focus on what's positive around you. You'll enjoy longevity and relative sanity. And you'll find that it's easier to be effective on a church staff or volunteer team. *You get more flies with honey* …Volunteers will be drawn to your ministry, and staff will want to work with you. What if you're not naturally a flexible and optimistic person? If you need your world to run according to a strict schedule without deviation, if you see things in black and white, if you tend to question things, and see the downside, you may struggle in media ministry leadership. You might try to change, to learn new ways to respond. Or you might find a flexible optimist who can join you in ministry. Partner with this person, and you'll complement one another's style. I've seen similar teams become ministry powerhouses!

Chaos

A disclaimer is necessary here, at the very beginning of this section, and not in fine print. If your media ministry is typical, planning is not a strong point. In fact, in my own experience, planning only became part of our operations for two reasons: (1) We suffered many kinds of failures as a result of poor (or nonexistent) planning, and (2) We were forced into it. But not exactly kicking and screaming. After five years of chaos, we were so worn out from our failures and from the chaos in general that we actually required very little coercion.

I am predisposed to poor planning. I am often unrealistic about how much time it takes to do things. I struggle to see the details in process, which means that while I have a clear vision of the end product or goal, I am sometimes blind to what it will realistically take to make it happen. I overestimate the amount of work that people, including me, can do in a given amount of time.

I believe these are dangers not only for me but also for many media ministry leaders. We are visual people. We don't have many models and mentors to learn from, except for those offering technical advice. We often must figure out issues of structure, process, and leadership on our own. This is in contrast to many of our church-work colleagues, who often have standardized practices to learn from, and many networking groups and colleagues to rely on for guidance. We in media ministry typically start out as a one-person-band, doing everything by ourselves for several years before adding substantial staff or volunteers. From this experience, we form our habits and our idea of how things work. And we often fail to change as our ministries grow, operating instead by the seat of our pants, long after that works, long after the ministry around us has ballooned into a complicated, often out-of-control mess. We have chaos.

Chaos is perhaps the biggest threat to a media ministry's ability to stay on purpose. Some of the reasons for this are listed in the paragraph above. Another reason is that church staff, in the worship area and among preachers who wait for Saturday night inspiration, are often simply not trained to plan ahead more than two weeks. Along with the general lack of understanding about media ministry, there is specifically a lack of understanding about just how long it takes to produce a short video or a graphics sequence or an audio clip for use in worship. Most experience in the area is limited to non-professional, home-based projects. "I put together Susie's birthday video in an hour and a half. Why should it take more than that for you to edit the Sunday school teacher recruitment video for this week's service?" Our work requires time, and far more time than most people realize. If we're trying to do better than "seat-of-our-pants," we must plan.

> We don't have many models and mentors to learn from, except for those offering technical advice. We often must figure out issues of structure, process, and leadership on our own.

Production Timelines for Planning

Use these as general rules of thumb when planning, and when explaining your time constraints to others in your church.

Video production. Using all-new video shot specifically for the project, edited on a non-linear system with very simple graphics and no animation or special effects... Not counting time for meetings, concepting, or scriptwriting. Average time to complete from start to finished product for worship: ten to fifteen hours per finished minute.

Graphics production. Basic graphics for a one-hour worship service including announcements, lyrics, Scripture and two to three miscellaneous graphics for sermon illustration ... Using pre-existing backgrounds with no creation of new backgrounds, including formatting of four to five images in Photoshop or similar program... Not counting time for meetings, concepting, proofreading, or design and art direction. From creation to a sequence ready to play in worship: five to ten hours.

The Triangle Tool

My husband works as an advertising creative director. He writes and comes up with ideas for commercials. A long time ago, he told me about something his friend, Robert—also an ad guy—had shared with him. It's The Good/Fast/Cheap Triangle, and it's one of the handiest tools I know in planning media ministry.

In media production, projects can be two of the following, and only two: *Good,* meaning the project is "on purpose" and meets the other principles in this book; it is of excellent quality, especially. *Fast,* meaning the project takes less than the average amount of time to produce—new graphics design in a couple of days, a video shot and edited and fully produced in a five-day week, etc. *Cheap,* meaning the project incurs no exceptional costs above and beyond the normal costs of doing ministry—no freelancers need to be hired to do the work (unless this is your normal practice), no fees have to be paid in order to obtain media (unless this is your normal practice). Costs also include the human variety: the toll exacted from our staff and volunteers. This type of cost is real, and is even more important than monetary costs. But it's often overlooked in ministry planning. Imagine that these three things each form one side of a triangle. The Good/Fast/Cheap Triangle.

We apply the Triangle when considering any media production project, choosing which TWO sides we'll use. Understand, and help others to understand, that you can almost never do a project that's Good *and* Fast *and* Cheap. When planning your project, which one can you give up? Is it okay to spend

> **Remember the Good/Fast/Cheap Triangle. And remember, you only get two!**

the extra money to hire a freelancer to shoot your stewardship campaign video, in order to get the quality you want, on schedule? In this scenario, you're giving up *Cheap* to get *Good* and *Fast*. Or is it okay for the project's production values to be a bit less than usual, in order to turn it around in short order with no additional expense? In this scenario, you're giving up *Good* to get *Cheap* and *Fast*. Or can you push a project's deadline back by a few weeks, in order to spend the time with your in-house resources to create a really effective video? In this scenario, you're giving up *Fast* to gain *Good* and *Cheap*. Or is it okay to press your volunteers into service for three weeknights in a row, in order to produce a great special event in seventy-two hours? In this scenario, you're giving up the human type of *Cheap* in order to get *Good* and *Fast*. You get the idea. The Good/Fast/Cheap Triangle is a helpful tool for planning *on purpose*.

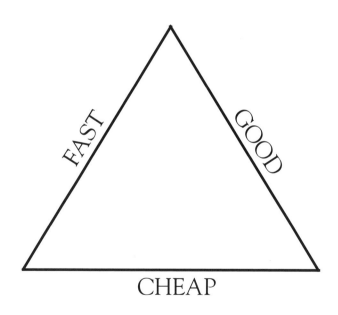

Three-Level Planning: Level One

I embraced planning partly because my supervisors applied it. Our congregation launched an extensive long-range or strategic planning process at the church-wide level and at the ministry level. In brief, it works like this: The Church Council sets somewhere between five and eight objectives each year for the church. Each objective has a measurable result, a due date, and an owner—the person responsible for ensuring the objective is achieved. Each objective is broken down into separate tasks (called action steps in some planning methods)—the specific steps necessary to accomplish the objective. Each task also has an owner and a due date. All of this information is compiled into an Excel spreadsheet.

I first saw this impressive document at a ministry directors' meeting. "Neat. Good idea for the Council to take this on. Sure will help guide the church, and keep the church focused on our purpose," I thought. Then our Senior Executive Director informed all of us that we would be offering a Long Range Plan for our ministry area, in the same way, too. Every year. From now on. And we'd be evaluated on our LRP success at our yearly performance review. I think I hyperventilated a little.

Then he unveiled the implementation schedule, which showed the dates when each ministry's LRP was due. Of course it would be too cumbersome to implement this grand new process across the board, all at once. So the plan was to launch it one ministry at a time over the course of a year, starting immediately. Guess which ministry got to go first? I guess the idea was to treat the "sickest patients" first. To be fair, or maybe naïve, I think our media ministry was tagged first in part because the executive team knew we'd embrace the process cheerfully, take it seriously, and be flexible enough to serve as the guinea pig, allowing the kinks to get worked out a bit. At any rate, at that point in the meeting, I was having trouble breathing.

But it all worked out more than okay. We've gone through the LRP process each year, and I'm a true believer. This is the first of the three levels of planning and is critical in staying on purpose. In fact, the Long Range Planning process may be the single most important strategy to keep your ministry working on purpose.

> The Long-Range Planning process may be the single most important strategy to keep your ministry working on purpose.

Three-Level Planning: Level Two

The second level of planning is mid-range planning. For our media ministry, this is roughly a three-month production schedule.

Toward the end of each quarter, we devote an extended meeting to a review of everything we know will need to happen that next few months. Concerts, special events, special worship services, videos, graphics, special lighting or staging for worship, and everything else we can think of. We break each piece into tasks, and assign each task to an owner. On the big projects, we set the timeline as a group. We begin with the project due date and plot each step from there, working backwards to the project's starting point. We try to schedule final due dates for two weeks out from the worship service. This allows us time for revisions and helps us stay flexible enough to respond to last-minute ideas and changes. This process applies to every aspect of media ministry, no matter how complicated or how simple.

Production Schedule

Create a color-coded document showing your production schedule, using an Excel spreadsheet. Assign each project a different color. Show who "owns" each step. Show all deadlines. Add details, as they're available, and update the document weekly, if necessary. Post it on your office door. Bring it to all your meetings. Check it daily. This tool alone provides a sense of control, and helps reduce the sense of chaos.

Protect Your Purpose

This mid-range planning protects your media ministry's focus on purpose in a couple of ways. First, it helps you articulate to others what you're doing, who's doing it, and when. This is valuable, especially when you're asked to do "just this one little PowerPoint® presentation for the aerobics class party next week," or to "run audio at the Little League meeting being held in the fellowship hall the week before Easter."

The schedule protects your media ministry's focus in another way. It literally *shows* others what your ministry's purpose is. Your purpose should be obvious and explicit in the types of projects that dominate your schedule. You'll need to articulate this in other ways, too. And you should have a clear and written-out policy on what type of projects are priorities for your ministry, which ones are not priorities but will be considered if the schedule allows, and which sorts of projects you will simply not have capacity or skills to do. The link here to purpose should be crystal clear: Your top priority should be projects that are directly related to your church's purpose and, therefore, to your ministry's purpose. Anything that

> Your top priority should be projects that are directly related to your church's purpose and, therefore, to your ministry's purpose.

falls outside of a direct correlation with your purpose should not be a top priority. You may do these projects, but they should come only when you're able to manage them without negatively impacting your top priority work. Any project that falls very wide of your purpose should not be on your list at all.

For our media ministry, 80–90 percent of our projects in any given month are directly linked to our purpose, usually via weekend worship. PowerPoint® presentations for an aerobics class or staff-time spent on a Little League meeting are so far from our core purpose that they cannot be priorities for us. This is not to say that your church, or mine, shouldn't do these sorts of events. But your media ministry will potentially touch every other ministry area, and will be called upon to produce media and events nearly 24/7. As much as you'd like to, and most of us in ministry would, you cannot do everything asked of you. Learn to prioritize and plan. And share that plan with others.

Propagate the Planning

Another good thing happens when you share your mid-range plan with others on your church's staff: They begin to see the value of planning, too. In some churches, most ministries already do great mid-level planning, working together to share resources, coordinate themed activities, and plan events that maximize purposeful use of facilities and minimize strain on staff and volunteers. But in many churches, this sort of planning doesn't happen. Pastors, ministry directors, and lay leaders are working hard to solve problems and take care of the day-to-day needs for the church. Each is generally going in his or her own direction most of the time. In fact, our very large church grew exponentially for ten years without much coordinated mid-level planning. Planning, or lack of it, isn't just an important issue for large churches, it's important for all churches. Often in churches of one-hundred members, 20 percent (or fewer) of the people do all of the ministry work—until they burn out, and then there is decline. Quarterly or mid-level planning should be done consistently in each ministry, and ministries should share their planning with one another early enough in the process that changes can be made to facilitate coordination.

Calm the Storm

Finally, mid-level planning literally calms that swirling wind of chaos, allowing us to stay focused on our ministry's purpose. How? Simply by showing us that it's really not as bad as we think it is, most of the time. The weekly deadlines for websites, worship graphics, videos, bulletins, newsletters, and all the rest can be a lot to manage, especially with an all- or mostly volunteer staff. Add to that mix all the events and special projects, including Christmas and Easter, and it's easy to see why media ministry servants are typically overwhelmed and stressed-out all year long. We tend to carry that around with us all the time, especially as the ministry leaders. In the back of our minds, it's not just this week's worship and bulletin that weigh on us. It's the web page reconstruction due next month, and the music director's ambitious new idea for the Christmas pageant, and the graphics that still need to be designed and created for the stewardship campaign dinner. It's insultingly easy to say, "just take it one day at a time." But thorough quarterly planning, plotted out on paper, shows you how to do just that. The production schedule shows you that, indeed, next week has no excess capacity; you can't take on another thing then. But the week after next, you will have met your deadline for the newsletter and you'll have two open days to work with the volunteer designer on those graphics.

Your ministry volunteers will benefit from this, too. They'll fall victim to the same sense of living in a constant hurricane if you do. I've seen this with my own team. We'll get a new assignment or decide to take on a project, and the chorus begins. "Are you kidding? Do you have any idea how much stuff we've got to do this month? We don't have time for one more thing!" (Note: lots of times, I'm either leading the chorus, or at least humming along.) Now, since we've become intentional about quarterly planning, we can look at the realistic picture, in black and white and color. Often we see that, even though we may sometimes feel overwhelmed and maxed out, we really can do more. This is an awesome gift that I don't want you to miss. You and volunteers will feel in control. You'll see that you really do have the critical things covered, that it really will all get done. You'll all sleep better at night. Put another way, you'll be salty. *You are the salt of the earth. But if the salt loses its saltiness, how can it be made salty again? It is no longer good for anything, except to be thrown out and trampled underfoot* (Matthew 5:13). I equate the salt in this passage with passion. Chaos drains us of our passion in ministry, but that passion seeps back in when we regain a sense of calm and control. But the best part of this gift is the fact that you will find you're able to do more of the work you love to do and, most importantly, that that work is daily helping your ministry to fulfill its purpose— God's purpose for it and for your church.

TECH TEAMS AS SMALL-GROUP MINISTRY

Small-group ministries are a fast-growing phenomenon in many churches. They're not new, of course. We read about house churches in the book of Acts, and we recall that Wesley's covenant groups were an important part of early Methodism. What's new, however, is the intentional way small groups are being defined as a critical part of the church's discipleship ministry. If your church is chasing after or already riding this bandwagon, consider how your tech teams might fit into the small-group model. Find out how your church defines a small group. Does your tech team fit that definition? If not, could you change them in some way—add new requirements, perhaps—to make them fit? Or are your small groups defined in a way that tech teams will simply not fit? I'm making no judgment or recommendation either way, just encouraging you to have this discussion with your church staff and leaders. It's important for two reasons: (1) Strong and effective ministries are cohesive, interconnected, and collaborative. Media ministries too often act and feel like the ugly duckling, disconnected from the rest of the church's work. Find ways to integrate your media ministry, and it will become stronger and more effective. (2) The spiritual formation of your volunteers is critical. Many of your volunteers might never consider joining a Sunday school class or small group. If there's an opportunity for you to "sneak" discipleship into their ministry work, you should take it!

> Chaos drains us of our passion in ministry, but that passion seeps back in when we regain a sense of calm and control.

Three-Level Planning: Level Three

The third level of planning is the nuts and bolts, daily and weekly planning we do to reduce purpose-squelching chaos. There are two key components to this type of planning. First, a staff person (or full-time, on-site volunteer) should be the central figure in your daily and weekly planning. This person should be at all weekday meetings with the pastors, music leaders, and other worship staff. This person must be a front line recipient of all last-minute changes. He or she must be immediately accessible and have access to the other worship staff. This is nearly impossible to manage from a distance. Your ministry can operate with mostly volunteers, but having a person on site, on staff, in all the important worship planning meetings is critical.

The second component of third-level planning is a strong communication structure, built upon the shoulders of your ministry's volunteer leadership. Your ministry should have a clear leadership structure. You'll need to build teams of volunteers, and each team should have a leader. If your church and ministry are large, you'll need to create units or divisions of multiple teams. For instance, if you have three camera teams, each responsible for running camera at one of your three worship services, you might consider creating a Camera Unit consisting of the three camera teams. This structure allows for growth and streamlines communication.

So, let's say you've got some sort of volunteer leadership structure already in place. Each of your teams has a Team Leader. If you have multiple teams, you may have Division Leaders or Unit Leaders, too. *Each of these leaders is critical in your Level-Three planning.* They should each be connected to that staff person who is present at all the weekday worship meetings. There should be a continual stream of information and communication between the staff person and these key leaders. *And,* these leaders should be connected in the same way to the persons on their teams. This should work the other direction, too. Volunteers should know their team leader. They should have his or her phone number and e-mail address. And they should feel comfortable sharing information with their team leader—concerns, questions, ideas for improving their ministry, and the joy and pain of their personal life. That same process should hold true throughout the line of sight, from volunteers to leaders to staff.

Think for a moment of an old cartoon ant farm. The ants scurry in lines from the gigantic picnic blanket to their hill home, carrying tidbits of picnic food with them; they then return immediately for more. It's a constant stream. Like industrious ants, your on-site staff person should be in weekly communication with the team leaders, who should be in weekly communication with the volunteers on their teams.

And picture, in the ant cartoon, a burly ant standing next to the constant stream, wearing a sergeant's hat and shouting encouragement through an ant-sized megaphone: "Keep it up, Charlie, you're doing great! Watch that watermelon, it's slipping! Move a little faster, Hilda…there ya go!" That ant is you.

The Mouse or a Meeting?

Use phone calls as often as possible, and rely on e-mail for basic factual information such as hymn numbers and verses, placement on the chancel of the children's choir, and so forth. Remember that e-mail is a terrible conveyor of emotion; misunderstandings, hurt feelings, and defensive reactions are often the result. So, as a general rule of thumb, use e-mail only for factual communication. The exception to this rule is to send a simple and immediate "thank you." If you need to address *any* issue that you have strong feelings about—a volunteer's botched graphics sequence or the audio person's harsh words to a vocalist—deal with it the good old-fashioned biblical way: in person, with grace. This is almost always harder in the short term, but is the best way for the long-term health of your ministry team.

Three-level plan now!

Even if your media ministry is still on the drawing board or in its infancy, start planning on three levels. Not planning until several years after our media ministry was born was a mistake that cost a lot in terms of misunderstandings with other ministries and stressed out volunteers. Whatever your scope of work, you'll avoid purpose-killing chaos if you plan!

In both small and large churches, the worship team involves multiple roles (preaching, music, altar or worship environment, stewardship, greeting/ushering, and communication in print or digital media), each with a weekly deadline. Perhaps your media ministry's planning will inspire the others to do the same. Perhaps your planning for worship will improve, allowing all of you to do more impactful, relevant worship. Show the worship leaders your planning documents, and show them how the deadlines you set for them will help you all succeed. Lead by example!

Opposition

I've shared the following story repeatedly with our teams, to help them—and me—remember that purpose trumps opposition nearly every time.

I joined the church's staff in order to launch our media ministry. For several years, I'd produced video projects for the church once or twice a year. We'd set up screens and projectors for these special occasions. But in 1997 a new sanctuary was designed. It would seat fifteen hundred people, and screens would be necessary to enable everyone to see. This gave us the opportunity to catapult our once-a-year video ministry into something that was an intrinsic part of the church. One small problem: Not everyone thought video should *be* part of the church.

There were many naysayers with various objections. I won't list them here, because I'm guessing that you've heard them all. One man was particularly vociferous and relentless in his opposition. Every time I saw him he had a new argument, and he never missed an opportunity to remind me of our impending huge mistake. As the building neared completion, I tried to avoid this man. Secretly, I wondered if he and the others were right, if we were making a mistake somehow. And I was certainly in over my head: I'd never done anything like this before, I had no experienced advisor to keep me out of trouble, and I had no real assurance that what we were doing would work.

What I did have, though, was a deep and profound sense of purpose for this new ministry, the support of the senior pastor, and a handful of persistent encouragers.

Our first services in the new building were on Christmas Eve. We designed very simple graphics for the services, based on classical art images of the Nativity. We used these for lyric backgrounds, Scripture, and the "welcome" page. They were beautiful and tasteful, and they helped create a wonderful feeling for our congregation and visitors. At the end of the night, after our 11:00 PM service, I was tidying up the tech booth when I noticed Mr. Opposition climbing the steps toward me. There was no escaping this confrontation.

As he walked up to me I saw tears in his eyes. "This was beautiful," he said. "I've never experienced Christmas like this. Everything on the screens helped make it more real and more wonderful than it ever was before. I didn't know it would be like this…I was wrong. Thank you." He walked away while I was still trying to figure out how to respond.

When faced with opposition, our human tendency is to immediately dismiss and defend. Instead, we should listen. Is there something in the criticism we should consider? Any little nugget that might actually make sense? Something we hadn't seen or thought of? In the case of Mr. Opposition, his criticisms sharpened my attention to purpose. When we planned that Christmas Eve, I was keenly aware of the skeptics who'd be sitting cross-armed in their seats, looking for every opportunity to prove their point: video in worship is crass, inappropriate, distracting, and unnecessary. We do things differently—better—because we listen to opposition.

It helps, too, to validate the critic: Acknowledge that screens *will* change the look of the old stone chapel. Commend the critic's faithful devotion to the Worship Committee, and express gratitude for his

> We do things differently—better—because we listen to opposition.

perspective. Thank her for sharing her viewpoint with you. Sometimes, opposition *expects* a defensive, dismissive reaction. There are some in our churches who have fallen into the rut of complaining and can't seem to climb out of it. After a while, others begin to see complainers as irrelevant. The rut gets deeper, and no one is willing to pull the complainer out. When we stop and listen and validate the complainers, we might just win a few converts.

Instead of defending your media ministry, explain it. In many churches, people don't really understand what media ministry can do. We resist what we don't understand. Memorize talking points, if that helps, so that you can explain the ways media ministry will help fulfill your church's purpose. Have ready a handful of specific examples that illustrate a direct link between media and purpose. "The Church Council's purpose statement says that we're to reach new people and teach them effectively. Graphics during the sermon will help people remember the pastor's points."

Gather up the encouragers, people who support media ministry, and enlist them as your team of "good gossipers." Stay in touch with them, bounce your ideas off them, and elicit their input. Make sure they understand the purpose connection of the ministry, and ask them to share it with others.

Finally, when opposition is in your way, take a tip from Nehemiah.

> *The king said to me, "What is it you want?"*
> *Then I prayed to the God of heaven, and I answered the king.*
> (Nehemiah 2:4–5a)

Pray, and persevere. Remember what happened next to Nehemiah? (Re-read this book for powerful wisdom on team-building and facing challenges!) If you know you're on the right track, stay on it!

Questions for Media Ministry Planning

(1) What are the unmet needs in the area around our church?

(2) What do we know about our community that might indicate God's purpose for us there?

(3) What are our church's strengths and resources?

(4) How might we leverage those strengths and resources to build God's kingdom where we are?

(5) What is the one thing that, if our church doesn't do it, will probably not be done?

(6) What do the people in our community see as our purpose?

(7) What do they see as the needs that a church might meet?

(8) What is already being done by churches in our area? These might be things we can cross off our list.

(9) What is the most important thing our church can do, stated as specifically as possible?

(10) How might we do this thing?

(11) Who exactly will be affected?

(12) What do we expect to happen as a result?

(13) What does God tell us to do?

(14) What is the purpose of our church?

(15) What is the purpose of our ministry?

(16) How can we use media to help fulfill the purpose of our ministry?

(17) How can we use media to help fulfill the purpose of our church?

CHAPTER TWO

Values

About two years into the life of our media ministry, I took a phone call from a friend within the church. "I've got a great opportunity for you guys to work on an awesome project—something that's a little different from what you normally do," my friend said. "And you'll be helping some people who really need help." I was interested. My friend was on the board of directors of a local non-profit agency serving troubled kids. They needed a video to show at a big fundraising event, and to use as a general fundraising tool. Sort of like the capital and stewardship campaigns we'd produced for the church.

Early on, as I was dreaming about what a church video ministry could be, I envisioned producing projects for many outside "clients," such as social service agencies, other churches, and non-profit organizations. They all need media, for fundraising or training or information, and few could afford high-quality video production. Saving Grace Productions could fill the gap, I reasoned. My friend's project would give us our start.

We shot and edited the video, and enjoyed the work. The agency was grateful for the cheap rates, and the video was effective. We felt satisfied that our efforts might really help some children. This outside project, however, was outside of our church's objectives. We spent many hours focusing on work that was important and necessary for this social service agency. But it was neither important nor necessary for the ministry of Saving Grace Productions. The outside client video had a negative impact on the projects we were producing for our church; it siphoned away our time and our attention.

⸙

That project was my mistake, but it illustrates the principle of values. Our congregation claims three core values: Transforming Lives,

Changing the Community, and Renewing Mainline Churches. Producing work for a secular agency, regardless of how compelling their cause or how desperate their situation, was outside of those values. Let's say that one of our values was Building Stronger Families, or Equipping Struggling Teens. Then the project might have made sense.

Isn't good work valuable for its own sake? What's wrong with taking the opportunity to help, wherever it's needed? How can I say the project was a mistake, when it really did help kids? It was not a mistake for the project to get done; it was just a mistake for our media ministry team to do it. It was a project of value. It was not, however, a project in line with our ministry's values.

In this chapter, we'll examine the principle of values. We'll start with a brief discussion of values—we'll look at what values are, how they're related to purpose, and why they're important. Then, you'll see how we apply the principle of values in our work within a video-based media ministry, with specific examples on the DVD accompanying this book. Next, you'll learn how to apply the principle of values in the way you form and operate your media ministry. Finally, you'll review a list of pointed questions.

Working within Your Values

> If your purpose is the overall *thing you're supposed to do*, your values are the *ways you'll do it*.

I really dislike the word, *values*. Sometimes, especially during political campaigns, I've felt like I've been batted over the head with values. Some folks seem to use the word as if it were a black-and-white matter, as if values were unchanging and universal. I don't see it that way. One dictionary defines values in this way: "the beliefs people have about what is right and wrong and what is most important in life, which control their behavior."[3] So, one person's set of values may be different than another's.

You might think of values as the strategies you use to fulfill your purpose. If your purpose is the overall *thing you're supposed to do*, your values are the *ways you'll do it*. What is most important for your ministry as you strive to fulfill your church's purpose? The answer to that question should "control your behavior" as a ministry.

As with the church's purpose, the pastor should articulate values for the staff, lay leaders, and congregation. Pastors should communicate this

---

[3] See Cambridge Advanced Learner's Dictionary, http://dictionary.cambridge.org

set of purpose-filling strategies quarterly in sermons, staff meetings, newsletters, on the website—using whatever means are available. And of course, the media ministry serves as the pastor's mouthpiece in this effort. Your work should reflect and reinforce the values identified by the church leadership and articulated by your pastor.

My own pastor, Rev. Adam Hamilton, has articulated the church's values consistently and often. (He uses the term *vision* rather than *values*.) Hamilton says, "Our three visions [values] are similar to our purpose. They reflect our preferred picture of the future. We hope, twenty-five years from now, to have seen thousands of lives changed, people having moved from non-religious and nominally religious to becoming deeply committed Christians. We hope to see the Kansas City area and beyond looking more like the Kingdom Jesus preached as a result of our presence. And we hope to see the mainline churches experiencing renewal and revitalization as a result of our presence."

CAVEAT: It's okay to do work outside of the confines of your church's defined values if that work won't negatively impact your ability to serve within the values. If you have the capacity to do some work that's not directly related to your values, go for it. For example, you may assist another church with the design and set-up of their new sound system, even though that doesn't fall squarely within your defined values. Or you might duplicate a DVD for another ministry or agency, even though that's not "on your list."

Work within your values. That statement may raise questions. What if my church doesn't have any stated values? If my church doesn't claim any values, per se, how can we get some? How do we know what they should be?

If your church has no stated values, try to determine why. It may be that the values are folded within a purpose statement. Some purpose statements are more detailed than others and go into line-by-line specifics about what the church will do. If this is the case in your church, dissect that purpose statement to find the values. If the purpose includes statements like the following, you've found your values:

- We will equip the families in our congregation to share their faith in the world.

- We will provide an enriching Christian environment for the children in our church and in our neighborhood.
- We will create affinity-based communities within our church, for weekly praise, worship, and celebration with like-minded people.

Each of these provides a strategic picture. Talk with the pastor and others about the purpose statement to clarify how you'll use it to prioritize your work. They might decide to follow your example; we can each benefit from setting priorities.

If the purpose statement is broad, without narrow objectives, ask the pastor or church council/board to work with you to discern what your church's values should be. This kind of focus is normally the pastor's task, though it is usually a collaborative endeavor with key leaders. Consider your church as aimed at its purpose, as if on a journey. Now, what are the best ways for *your church, your ministry* to get there? What are your strengths? What are your liabilities? What will make sense to your community? What has God revealed to you about God's specific expectations of your church?

Determining values from scratch is a collaborative process that should include laity, staff, the church council, and pastor. Seek perspectives from people in your community, too. Does the mayor see a capability in your church that you don't see? Could directors at local mission agencies provide a clarifying perspective? People outside your congregation may be most helpful in identifying purpose-aimed pathways. Another way to identify values is to identify what they *shouldn't* be. The process of elimination. You might start there, ruling things out, making it clear that those things are off the table.

Why are values so important? Why can't we just identify our purpose and move on? As I said before, values function as the strategies we use to fulfill our purpose. Without those strategies, our journey toward purpose would be random, meandering. Values are the road map; when you work within your values, it's as if you're walking within the lines on the map. Put another way, values provide the *how* on our way to reaching the *why*.

Your church's values give shape and clarity to its purpose. They also provide the standards for prioritization. This is critical for media ministries. Media ministries, perhaps more than any other type of ministry, can quickly become overwhelmed with the *important*. Graphics for weekend worship are important. The video sermon illustration is important.

So is the webcast, the video for children's Sunday school, and the missions ministry slide show. We're blessed with very powerful tools. In part because of that power, our work tends to snowball. To put it another way, success leads to opportunity. You produce a great

> Success leads to opportunity, but opportunity can lead to destruction.

video for worship, and the missions ministry director realizes that a video could help her recruit more volunteers. And she's right. Soon, the children's department is asking for a fun graphics presentation for the kids at Easter. The children and parents love it, of course. If you use these powerful tools well, you'll help your church and its ministries succeed. Others will see that, and will want some themselves! Success leads to opportunity.

But opportunity can lead to destruction. Because you're doing good work with powerful tools, opportunities to do *more* work multiply. Soon your ministry has more opportunities than it has capacity. If you don't prioritize those opportunities, you may find that you've become unsuccessful. I can look back on the outside project situation now and appreciate the irony. I couldn't do that at the time. Better avoid the situation altogether: Work within your values!

Applying Values in Your Ministry's Work

What does the principle of values mean in the work you produce? How do values affect the way you do what you do?

Values are closely linked to purpose, as we've seen. As with the principle of purpose, the principle of values should apply in just about everything we produce. Our videos, graphics, newsletters, and web content should each consistently underscore our church's values. If our values are to influence our behavior as a church, then our media ministry must show the congregation what that behavior looks like and tell them why it's important. If values are the road map we follow on our way to fulfilling our purpose, then our media ministry must inspire the congregants to stay on the right path. Let's look at some of the ways we can show, tell, and inspire.

First, a word of warning for what *not* to do: Don't reserve your emphasis on values for special times, such as the annual Stewardship Campaign, Missions Month, Discipleship Weekend, or Teacher Recruitment Sunday. There will be certain times each year when the events or sermon topics align perfectly with your church's values. It's easy to see ways to show, tell, and inspire at those times. But if you communicate your church's values only once or twice a year, you're missing opportunities.

Here's an example. Let's say one of your church's values is "Discipleship through Bible Study for Families." Your church places high importance on home-based biblical study for every family in the church. You've purchased curriculum and outlined training sessions for parents. The Sunday school leaders have created a booklet of activities for every age, to go along with the study. The pastor has written children's messages to reinforce the curriculum in worship each week. It's an awesome program and an effective strategy to propel your church toward its purpose. The program kicks off each year in August.

So what's your task? Produce a great video or slide show or graphics presentation or newsletter article or web piece for the kickoff. Show how the "Bible Study for Families" program has impacted congregants' lives. Show how fun it is to play and learn together as a family. Help participants tell how easy it is to use the curriculum. Tell the congregation how to sign up. Inspire them to make this a priority in their lives by coaxing them to understand why it's a priority for your church. Do all these things, but not just for the kickoff weekend.

Evaluate your work to find ways to reinforce the church's values in the work you do, to the greatest degree possible. Perhaps that means a "Bible Study for Families" column in the monthly newsletter. Or a direct link from the church's website home page. Could you project the Bible memory verses each week in the sanctuary as people gather for worship? How about a family photo slide show during the offering once a month, featuring the kids' Bible study crafts? When you determine what you'll produce each week or each month, intentionally look for ways to direct the congregation's attention to the church's values.

There's another way to reinforce values in your work. The previous example offers ways to reinforce values directly. But you can find ways to reinforce values indirectly, too. Perhaps you produce a video for missions, featuring the people who traveled to help the refugees from a hurricane. When you interview these volunteers, ask them to describe how their experience in "Bible Study for Families" affected their decision to go on the trip. Did the Bible study deepen their conviction that Christians are meant to serve in this way? Did the study help them to be more open to prompting of the Holy Spirit? Did they feel compelled to live out their faith in front of their children, because of the study they'd completed together? A video touting missions could, in this way, serve double duty as a powerful values reminder for the congregation.

Can you imagine other ways to indirectly reinforce your church's values, embedding the message in other media projects? A Sunday school teacher recruitment video might include this reference: A mom explains how easy and rewarding it is to teach Sunday school, and how the Bible Study dispelled her misconception that sharing Scripture with kids was beyond her ability. Here's another example: You're writing a newsletter or web page article on your church's music ministry. Ask the choir director how understanding Scripture helps the choir to communicate in worship. Interview choir members who can tell how their family Bible study experience has enriched their role in leading worship. When you directly and indirectly reinforce your church's values for the congregation, those values become a part of the church's culture (see chapter 3).

> Nothing is more inspirational than testimony from someone you know, or someone you feel is "just like me."

Notice a common thread in these examples. They're personal. They feature real people from your congregation showing and telling their peers in the pews why your church's values are important. Nothing is more inspirational than testimony from someone you know, or someone you feel is "just like me." Be on the lookout for these folks. Ask around among the church staff and laity for references. Make a note when you meet someone who might have a story to share. Save letters and e-mails from potential interviewees.

Finally, when it's time for your next capital campaign or annual stewardship drive, you should focus very clearly on values. Stay on message. Show and tell the congregation why your church's values are important and how they are strategically related to your purpose.

Applying Values in the Formation and Operation of Your Ministry

My right eyelid develops a twitch every October. In some years, the left side joins in for fun. This irritating phenomenon is caused by stress or, to be more specific, it's caused by (scary music, howling wind, diabolical laughter goes here) *the budget process!* At my church, we submit our requests for the next year's budget in October. We spend a few weeks hashing out the details until we're finally finished, usually sometime around Thanksgiving. When I crash completely on the Friday after T-day, it's not just from the tryptophan.

The application of values can make ministry easier to manage and more effective. In this section, we'll examine three challenges we face in the application of values. At the end of the section, I'll share more specifically how this principle impacts your ministry, even The Budget.

Three things tend to get in our way as we strive to reinforce our church's values.

(1) Lack of Focus

(2) Lack of Unity

(3) Lack of Boldness

Lack of Focus

In the previous chapter on purpose, I shared with you how important long-range planning has become for me. Values are a critical part of that planning. Values give shape and clarity to our church's purpose. When we do long-range planning, we measure proposed plans against our values. Do they line up? Are the plans on track with our values? Can we see a direct link between values and the objectives we set for ourselves? We rule out things that don't line up, aren't on track, and don't link directly with our values. That long-range planning process sharpens our focus.

It reminds me of the bizarre experience we have at the optometrist's office, with our foreheads pressed up against that strange black metal contraption with all the flippy lenses. The doctor's ultra-calm voice says, "Please look at the chart on the wall. Which is clearer, this one, or this? A or B? The first, or second? All right. Now which is clearer, this or this? The first one, or the second? A or B?" By eliminating options that are a bit fuzzy, you narrow vision into clear focus.

Focus allows us to be effective, to be successful. When we focus, we are able to prioritize. We do work that drives our ministry and our church toward its purpose, and we say "no" to projects that veer off into some other direction, even if they're really fun and worthwhile projects. I learned this one the hard way, as you recall. Focus, as the optometrist's office illustrates, is not just being able to see, it's being able to see clearly.

> Focus is not just being able to see, it's being able to see clearly.

This is one tricky aspect of focus. As you begin using your media tools more effectively, and as opportunities multiply, you may find yourself staring at a long list of projects that *all* line up with your church's values. Which is fine, unless you don't have the resources to successfully complete all those great projects. You've set the priorities that determine what types of projects are on the table. But you'll probably need to narrow the list even further to determine which projects stay on the table, and which ones get taken away. You'll need to create some sort of process to determine which of the values-oriented projects you'll do. You might use a first-come, first-served system. Or let a team of staff and laity decide. Or plan a way for each ministry area to get its turn throughout the year.

Roller Coaster Ride

If you're not living in this spot now, you probably will be soon. If you've been there recently, you'll probably be back in due time. It's a cyclical thing with media ministries. We do good work, are asked to do more good work, and pretty soon have more work than we can handle. We struggle and sweat and shuffle resources around, train more volunteers and figure out how to increase our ministry's capacity. We breathe a sigh of relief, roll up our sleeves and dig in to do good work. We're asked to do more good work…You know where this is leading. Just know that this is the roller coaster you're on, and enjoy the ride!

We're in ministry, and we want to serve. We enjoy our work, and we want to do all we can. But, if there's one mistake I hope to help you avoid, it's the urge to do it all. A scattershot approach, even when rooted in good intentions and based on your church's values, will dilute your focus and set you up for failure. Decide what you'll do and what you won't do based on your church's values. Do consistent long-range planning to make sure that your work is directly linked to the values. Prioritize those projects, and get help making that happen if you need it.

Lack of Unity

May the God who gives endurance and encouragement give you the same attitude of mind toward each other that Christ Jesus had, so that with one mind and one voice you may glorify the God and Father of our Lord Jesus Christ. (Romans 15:5–6)

The second thing that gets in the way of values is lack of unity among staff and lay leaders in the church. If you align your work with the church's values, but another ministry area pursues a different course—

even if that course is roughly aimed at the church's purpose—your church may be less effective than it would be if all the ministries were on the same track. This works on multiple levels. Your volunteers should know and understand the values of your church and should be willing to relinquish personal or group agendas in order to pursue those values together. The same holds true for your colleagues in other ministry areas. You're running different ministries, so of course the tactics will differ from ministry to ministry. But you should all be lining up your tactics with the church's values.

It's difficult sometimes in churches to require people to limit their ministry. That's what it can feel like, when we're asked to narrow our focus on a specific set of values. When we focus on one set of values, we necessarily set aside other values. Remember the dictionary definition? Values control our behavior, so when values are established that are new to us, we must adjust our behavior. We don't generally like that kind of change. Especially in established denominations—where we're striving to open up, to reach out, to revitalize our churches—it can seem wrong to place restrictions on ideas for ministry. But in the end we are more powerful and compelling when we focus *together* on the same things. If as individual churches we can figure out how to do this, then as the Church, we can do a better job of bringing glory to God.

Lack of Boldness

The third thing I see as an obstacle to the principle of values is hesitation, or lack of boldness. It's a bit risky to put down on paper two or three values, riskier still to plan and organize your work around them. It seems we're sometimes hesitant to claim territory, to say, "This is what we're going to do, and here's how we're going to do it." I'm not certain why some leaders fear risk. Perhaps we're worried about putting all our eggs in a couple of baskets and then failing. Perhaps we fear offending persons or groups of people. Perhaps we're unsure about what happens next, if we're successful.

But for whatever reasons, we hold back. We might have staff and volunteers who would gladly do the hard work of zeroing in on a well-defined set of values and would stride arm-in-arm together on the narrow path toward purpose. But if we hesitate, we are lost. In mainline churches, especially, we seem to stand with the stake in our hands, scratching the surface, unwilling to ram it into the ground, too hesitant to mark out the path with certainty. We have strong foundations and rich traditions of faith; we must learn to be bold.

The church budget intersects with each of the pitfalls I've outlined above, and this offers one last example of the importance of values. The budget process in my own ministry has become easier each year as our church has focused more and more on our set of three values. As we meet to hammer out the budget, we continually ask the question, "How does this help us communicate the church's values?" My colleagues in every other ministry do the same, so we're unified in our focus. And, when we publish the budget, with numbers—the tithes and offerings of our congregation—representing values-based ministry, we've stated our intentions rather boldly.

If we do our work well, the church's values become almost intuitive for the congregation, just as the purpose does. Values become part of the church's culture.

Questions for Media Ministry Planning

(1) What are our church's values?

(2) How can we use media to directly reinforce these values for the congregation, showing and telling them why these values are important?

(3) How can we use media to inspire the congregation to pursue these values as individuals and as a church body?

(4) What are the ways we can use media to indirectly reinforce our church's values, helping those values to become part of the church's culture?

CHAPTER THREE
Culture

The website's home page clicked and jittered onto my computer screen, little bits at a time. It took my eyes a moment to adjust. There was a lot happening, visually, on this site. The first thing that hit me was the use of many different colors. Remember in seventh-grade art class when you learned about the color wheel? Remember the natural rules of thumb about using color, how some shades contrast pleasingly with one another and others just clash? This website was clashing all over the place. The next assault came in font form. Swoopy scripts slammed up against chunky newsprint styles, with cartoonish juvenile type crammed in for good measure. Every text box and every background was gradient, an attempt to give images dimension. And every font had a hefty drop shadow. There were photos ranging from studio headshots to grainy amateur snapshots; recognizable pop art, cropped for the site; and original graphic compositions shoehorned onto the home page. "What a mess," I said to myself "I'm glad our church's site doesn't look like this." And that is precisely the point of the principle of culture.

The website described above is from a church in the area where I live. It is, from what I can tell, a growing congregation with many programs. They're broadcasting, bringing in guest speakers and artists, building new buildings, adding new members. Websites generally reflect something about the church, and to me this website looks cheesy, cluttered, and cheap. But my opinion is irrelevant; I'm not, nor will I ever be, a member of this church. For the people who call this church "home," it is a dynamic, appealing congregation that is jam-packed with activities and features a different speaker or entertainer nearly every week, and the website accurately reflects that. This church emphasizes different things—it has a different personality—than my own church does, and that is reflected in its website, worship graphics, video production, and direct mail pieces. The media ministry reflects the culture of the church.

In this chapter, we'll start with a brief discussion of culture and examine why it's important. Then, you'll see how we apply the principle of culture in our work within a video-based media ministry, with specific examples on the DVD accompanying this book. Next, you'll learn how to apply the principle of culture in the way you form and operate your media ministry. Finally, you'll review a list of pointed questions. It's my hope that these will become a resource for you, and that over the years they'll help you apply the principle of culture in your ministry.

Reflecting Your Congregation's Culture

Part of the job of our media ministry is to accurately reflect our individual church's culture. In order to effectively communicate to our congregations, we must speak their language. We must communicate in ways that feel real and resonate with the people in the pews. *Authentic* is an overused word, but authenticity is critically important in our work. You've probably had experiences like the one described above. You've visited a church or website that reflects a particular church culture, one that's different from yours. That's a great thing, as long as the culture reflected is real, resonant, and authentic to that congregation.

Your church has a personality, whether you've identified it or not. We tend to prefer spending time with people who are somewhat like us, so demographics inevitably shape our congregations. We can usually see one or two common threads running through our church membership. Age, race, and socio-economics are the easy ones to pick out, but there are others. Political beliefs, religious doctrine, and a sense of shared tradition often form common threads, too. In some churches, diversity is actually a common thread. Increasingly, churches are racially diverse, creating a whole new kind of strength and culture in those congregations.

> A big part of our task is to communicate to the people who are there every weekend. We must know who they are. We must understand how they communicate.

What is the culture of your congregation? Sometimes it's tough for us to lift this up—it's like looking in the mirror. We may wish we were a bit different. Many of us wish *we* could say our congregation is more racially diverse, for instance. But the principle of culture is important because a big part of our task is to communicate to the people who are there every weekend. We must know who they are. We must understand how they communicate. How do they get their information? How do they share with others? What sort of things do they read, hear, or watch? What sorts of images draw them in? These are important questions for us.

What happens if we ignore them? What's wrong with communicating in new ways to the same old folks? Let's look at a few examples of what can go wrong when we disregard the principle of culture.

- Example: Emergent culture churches, with media wallpaper, media for effect, and a media creating environment. Information is minimal, not highly produced. If this style of worship is not a good match with the church's culture, worship might seem irreverent, un-serious, careless, trendy, or shallow to the congregation. Their college-age grandchildren, however, might think it's great!

- Example: A church produces a funny video promoting its Advent activities. The pastor is a holiday ham, mugging for the camera, dressing up in wacky Santa suits and generally behaving like a goofball. In some church cultures, this would be a blast for the congregation, and very effective marketing. In other churches, the congregants would be very uncomfortable with the pastor's lack of reserve. Folks might walk out that morning with a bitter taste.

- Example: Sermon starters that are edgy and confrontational are the norm. Some folks appreciate the challenge and the up-front-ness of this technique. But in the wrong culture this can alienate people. It might be perceived as offensive to some, and others might simply resent the attempted manipulation.

Why shouldn't we push a little? Our tools get more fun and innovative every year, so why shouldn't we use them to their potential? We can both speak to our culture and learn to speak in new ways. In the next chapter, we'll look at how and why we should push at the edges in our ministry. But culture is critical, and our ministries suffer when we ignore that fact. Here are just a few ways:

- When we ignore our church's culture, and use the wrong "language," it can feel as if we're shoving something down the congregation's throat, devaluing their language and devaluing them. It creates opposition to media ministry and gives people a reason not to like it.

- When we ignore our church's culture, we make it difficult for our pastor to succeed. Pastors can't preach God's word as powerfully when they're uncomfortable with the way we're using media. We serve as their megaphone, and they must feel good using it. When we disregard our church's culture, we might actually damage the pastor's credibility with the congregation.

- When we ignore our church's culture, our ministry becomes less effective, period. It's as if we're making a lot of noise, but no one's listening. And in the end, we damage our ministry. When we try to force the congregation to understand our foreign language, they may eventually decide to pull the plug. Literally.

Some productions may be great for the media team itself, but we lose in the end if we're not effective.

Applying Culture in Your Ministry's Work

Here are some examples of how we've applied the principle in our media ministry at Resurrection, reflecting our church's unique culture:

- We carefully choose interview subjects who are articulate. In our setting, they are expected to be "experts." We must appeal to our somewhat cerebral congregation. This congregation is sensitive to anything that might feel manipulative, and it gives attention more freely to people who are well-informed and authoritative.

- The media team uses a lot of testimonials, or interview subjects who are simply sharing their own perspective or their experience. These literally reflect the culture back to the congregation.

- Text for graphics in worship and on video for worship is limited to a set of clean, simple, classical fonts from our stylebook.

- Backgrounds and other graphic elements are kept fairly simple, too.

○ Classical art and clean art direction form the basis for graphics.

○ One visually-strong piece functions as an anchor, and we pull elements from that piece for use in name supers, backgrounds, and other graphic applications. Visuals are cohesive, easy to grasp immediately.

○ The look is not edgy or controversial; we need to appeal to non- and nominally-religious.

○ Overall style is tasteful and classic to appeal to a congregation of mostly well-educated suburbanites.

○ Example: *Path of Wisdom* sermon series on Proverbs.

 – We purchased stock photo of a path through autumn trees.

 – We used the path image for bulletin, banners in the sanctuary, and as a main "welcome" graphic on screen as the congregation entered.

 – We used a single maple leaf for lyrics and Scripture.

 – We used a swatch of the leaf, made transparent, as the lower-third bar for name supers for worship I-mag and on video interview clips.

 – We used all of the above for graphics in the stewardship video played during worship.

○ We use effects in video and graphics sparingly; our congregation is not impressed by effects and has a low "cheesiness" threshold.

○ We use video sermon illustrations to make biblical concepts relevant and accessible, without being condescending. Example: Sermon series *Lessons from the Farm*, on growing in the Christian life.

 —We shot beautiful footage of rural scenes; cornfields, garden weeds, tractors spreading seed and fertilizer, manure spreader.

 —The scenes resonated with the congregation, many of whom had childhood ties to farming through grandparents.

 —This theme helped the congregation to be open as the pastor taught, using powerful and rich farm metaphors for Christian discipleship.

—The use of media in this series was incredibly effective; the congregation reported that they "got it," and were able to understand the sermon concepts more clearly.

—The uniqueness of the media images in this series helps the congregation to remember the concepts better, too.

— We don't experiment much. If so, we try in advance to determine if it will work or not. Our congregation has many skeptics, who would lose patience if we did too much edgy or experimental work. They expect media in worship to be meaningful and relevant and not to get in the way of their learning and worship. When it does, we've failed.

Some examples of ways to apply the principle of culture in other church settings:

- For video interviews, use people who will appeal to the congregation. If you're using experts, they should be drawn from the church's own culture.
  - As you're planning, ask, "To whom would the congregation listen on this subject? Where would they themselves turn?"
  - It might be local politicians, college professors, schoolteachers, business owners, civic leaders, or people from professional disciplines.
  - You're not producing the six o'clock news. Your experts should be people that the congregation will trust and to whom they'll pay attention.
- For video testimonials, use people from the congregation! The people sitting next to us on the church pew are a powerful witness. We have a lot in common, so their perspective is relevant.
- For text and graphics, establish a stylebook.
  - A stylebook is simply a manual—a list of do's and don'ts.
  - It should specify anything that's important in your setting— colors, fonts, font size, images that are okay to use and ones that aren't (in our setting, for instance, we don't use clip art), animation, effects, all the little details that make a difference in your work.

- In churches where the culture is young or urban, media ministries can use more trendy, effect-heavy, experimental graphics and videos. In these settings, it may work to use unusual fonts, humor, parody, and looser production values. These congregations may respond positively to more "in your face" and overtly challenging styles. These churches are rarities in the established denominations; if you're in one, lead the way for the rest of us!

- In churches where the culture is more traditional, older, or more rural, a simple style typically works best.
  - Here, it's often effective to use photos as backgrounds, along with simple graphics and few effects.
  - These congregations may appreciate a sense of natural beauty and restrained style.
  - Showiness often backfires for media ministries in more traditional church cultures.

- Find ways to lift up the unique culture of your congregation, to celebrate it with photo slide shows, graphic sequences, or video presentations.
  - If your church culture centers around families and children, for instance, is there a way you could feature kids' artwork in a graphics sequence before the worship service once each month? Perhaps you could work with the children's ministry to coordinate artwork that ties into the pastor's sermon theme. Or use shots, either stills or video, of the church community's activities over the last month.

- Is your congregation older, more hesitant about media, even resistant to its presence in worship? Feature longtime members of the church in your media as often as you can. Their perspective is valuable, and it will affect their peers.
  - If possible, find a few positive and articulate long-timers to interview on camera for your stewardship or capital campaign.
  - Or show lots of their beautiful and wise faces in a graphics sequence showing highlights from the last year.
  - We like to see ourselves raised up in this way, whether we admit it or not. The next best thing for most of us is to see the "person next door" raised up.

- You can deflate the puffed-up resistance to media bit by bit, if you enlist the help of friends of the resistance. Find folks who are not resistant or who are the least resistant, and invite their participation. They'll help you lead for change. This may not be a subtle tactic, but it really works.

• If you face resistance to media in your church: Take one small step at a time. Introduce media slowly.

- You may show a video once or twice a year, typically at stewardship campaign time, for two or three years.

- Add graphics for lyric support at one service each month, and later increase that to one service each weekend. Don't try to do it all at once.

- At our church, we hauled in big-screen TVs, projectors, and folding screens for nearly seven years before we created a production team and made the ministry official. We showed videos first for a capital campaign, the stewardship campaigns, then another capital campaign, then for a few church-wide events. These videos helped the congregation understand our values.

- We did one production a year for about four years. By the time we started the ministry and bought our first equipment in 1998, we were hauling in equipment two or three times a year.

- Let your congregation get used to media in worship, and give yourself the time to learn the ropes. You may get impatient, but your ministry and your church will benefit from a slow and deliberate buildup.

Applying Culture in the Formation and Operation of Your Ministry

There are other website evaluations I could offer, in addition to the one that launched this chapter. There are visits to websites that I've envied, with beautiful or innovative or engaging graphics and video. And more than website visits, there are visits to churches where I've had that very human "their-grass-is-greener" reaction. You know the feeling and the thoughts that run through your mind. They go something like this:

This is a good room. Better than ours. Their projector is brighter. And they have those shades to control the ambient light. Bet their budget is twice what I've got. They must have a full-time graphics designer; look at that stuff. They must spend a fortune on stock photography, too. And there hasn't been a single mistake. All run by paid staff, I'm sure. This service is back-to-back cool media. Our pastor would never agree to use text in the sermon like that, or videos. We never get to do fun stuff like this.

The greener-grass syndrome stems from a lack of appreciation for our church's unique culture. That's the second of three pitfalls we face as we strive to reflect our church's culture. They are:

(1) Lack of understanding of our church culture

(2) Lack of appreciation of our church culture

(3) Lack of understanding of communication in that culture

Lack of Understanding of Culture

The growth of our church is due in part to pastor Adam Hamilton's clear-eyed understanding of culture. Before the church had even met for the first time, he had studied the area where it would be located. More importantly, he studied and carefully considered the people and their unmet needs. He describes that process and the conclusions he made:

> When we began the Church of the Resurrection, our aim was not to convince other Christians to leave their churches to join ours. The people we were seeking to reach would be the 50 percent of the population that was not actively involved in other congregations. Some were never churched—nonreligious. Most had some exposure to church and the Christian faith while growing up, and perhaps had some kind of faith, but they were not actively involved in a church and likely not living their faith daily. We tried to understand what they were like. What kept them from being involved in a church? What questions kept them from making a commitment to the Christian faith? What were the issues in their lives that clearly pointed to their need for the gospel or the church? In our particular community, the demographics pointed towards a population that was very well educated, fairly successful, and, if they had grown up going to church, likely attended a mainline church. In addition a large number of them had children. All of these were factors in the way we "did" church.

What exactly is the unique culture of the people in your church? How can you identify it? This goes deeper than just saying, "We're a group of Christians from suburban Omaha." You must intentionally learn the key things

> Spend a little time studying and thinking about your congregants; develop a realistic understanding of who they are.

that your congregants share in common. The hometown is a given; you must find out more.

Start by looking around. What can you tell from the folks walking in the door on Sunday morning? How many kids are there in Sunday school? In the nursery? In the youth group? Take a look at the church's database or member list. Can you spot any trends there? Do people tend to live in the same neighborhoods, or types of neighborhoods? Does a significant percentage live in apartments or in assisted living centers? Do you see most listings without kids, or with kids who now live away from home? Or are there young children listed for many of the families? Have you conducted surveys or polls of the congregation to find out more about them? Could you use a survey to learn what level of education is most common? Could you determine what types of jobs are most common among your members? What about the data for financial giving to the church—what might you learn there? Again, can you spot any trends that might shed light on the church's culture? Spend a little time studying and thinking about your congregants; develop a realistic understanding of who they are. Understand your church's culture.

Lack of Appreciation for Culture

I must admit that I fall easily into the greener-grass trap. When I visit churches where the culture is predominantly African-American, I envy their vibrancy and out-loud spirit. I imagine how fun it would be for our camera operators to shoot that choir, those exuberant faces, how awesome it would be to help create such actively engaging worship experiences. I envy churches where media is used in a more edgy way, where the ministry team pulls out all the stops, and where the congregation welcomes effects and experimental techniques. In these church cultures, the tolerance of risk is high for media ministries; the congregations expect to be pushed and wowed each week. What a challenging and invigorating ministry environment! Inevitably, in my own creative sessions with staff and volunteers, somebody has a great idea that's just on the edge. It's disappointing, sometimes, to have to bat these ideas down; but they usually won't work in our church's weekend worship. Our culture expects to be pushed in more cerebral ways; they tend to find media that's very edgy to be distracting and irritating.

In some churches, most of the congregants were born around the time I was graduating from college and getting my first job in TV. Whatever you call them—Gen-Y or Emergent or Young Adults—their culture is particular to them. I love visiting these churches, where media has skipped over a generation, where it functions in a totally new way. In most mainline churches, we're still struggling to use media as a way to inform and educate. In many twenty-something churches, they've already zoomed past that function; media in these settings functions to create an environment, a mood, to inspire a feeling or attitude. The on-screen text for lyrics in a lot of these churches is incredibly basic.

In one leading church in California, hundreds of twenty-something young adults worshiped in a concrete-floor tent with an excellent (if grungy) band. There were some basic theatrical lights on the band, a little color but no motion lighting—nothing fancy. There were projected lyrics for worship and the played-back sermon from the main sanctuary service earlier that day. The lyrics were a basic font on a plain black background. No photos, no colors, no art, nothing. As if to say, "Sing the words, and don't think about anything else. Just see the words and let them go through you as you worship God. Nothing else should matter in this moment." Wow. How freeing it was. It felt to me like pure worship, focused on the right thing. All the extraneous had been stripped away. "This is *real*," I thought to myself. And it is indeed real for that culture. In the culture of my home church, it would feel wrong, cheap, half-hearted, and distracting.

I love my church. I understand its culture in part because I am of that culture. I appreciate the exuberance of African-American worship, and the innovation of edgy-media churches, and the pared-down sensibility of twenty-something worship. But I treasure and admire the well-educated, high-achieving, deep-thinking culture in my own congregation most of all. It's a privilege to find ways each week to communicate the gospel to (and with) them.

Lack of Understanding of Communication in the Culture

> He told them another parable: "The kingdom of heaven is like a mustard seed, which a man took and planted in his field. Though it is the smallest of all seeds, yet when it grows, it is the largest of garden plants and becomes a tree, so that the birds come and perch in its branches." (Matthew 13:31–32)

Matthew, Mark and Luke all record Jesus' beautifully simple parable of the mustard seed. This is one of the first passages of Scripture I remember learning. And I remember feeling that rush of awareness when, during second-grade Sunday school class, I *got it*. I understood—as much as a seven-year-old can—the lofty concept of God's kingdom, and that I was supposed to be part of it. For me, one of the most precious qualities of Scripture is its ability to transcend time and place, to always communicate in the culture. The parable of the mustard seed appealed to me and made sense to me as a child, and does so even more today. And what about the disciples, who were gathered around listening to Jesus' string of parables that day? He communicated directly to them, using their own language, tapping into their perspective, aware of their needs. Soil, weeds, yeast, fishing nets, lost coins, lost sheep, lost sons, harvest time, wedding feasts, and mustard seeds. These were the things of real life in that time and place.

Okay, so you understand your church's culture, and you appreciate it for what it is. Now, how do you communicate with and in that culture? Again, it takes a little research. First, what is the overall communication style of this culture in our society? The people in that cool California tent service communicate differently from the suburban mom in Omaha. How do they use media? Is it mainly for information? Entertainment? Background noise for their day-to-day lives? When they need to communicate something to someone, are they more likely to pick up the phone, write a letter, meet face-to-face, send an e-mail, or text message from their phone? How do they tend to receive information about the world? Do they watch the evening news every night? Is CNN their computer startup page? Do they read the newspaper daily, and newsmagazines weekly? Do they log onto a forum, zine, chat room, or blog every morning? What trends do you see that might help you create media that feels right for this culture? Should it be text-heavy or image-oriented? Should information come in short bits and pieces, like the scrolling ticker on the lower third of the cable newscasts? Should it be simple and bold, like a magazine ad? Should it move by the congregation quickly, or should it have time to sink in slowly? What sort of design elements most closely matches what they're used to seeing? Avant-garde, classical, or pretty-as-a-Hallmark-card?

You may be leading a ministry in a church where you are *not* of the culture, where you create media for people who are not so much like you. You have a special challenge. You may need to periodically return to what you learn about your church's culture, in order to remember to whom you're talking. You may need to bat down your own ideas often, in order to focus on ideas that will work better in your setting. You're creating media not to please yourself, but for the culture of the congregation you serve. This is one case where you really must give the people what they want.

Questions for Media Ministry Planning

(1) What is the culture of this church?

(2) How do people in this culture communicate with each other?

(3) How do people in this culture receive information?

(4) What stylistic elements are common in the communication of this culture?

(5) Does our media in worship "look" like the congregation?

(6) Do congregants recognize themselves in the media they see in church?

CHAPTER FOUR
Vision

In 1997, a former drug-addicted, alcoholic, homeless man named Garrett (not his real name) changed the way I thought and felt about ministry. He showed me how perseverance works and what courage looks like. He demonstrated for me that strange phenomenon: change. It's as if he held it up for me like a prism and slowly turned it around, revealing every different aspect of it. Garrett showed me the power of change, the pain of change, the drudgery of change, the beauty of change, and the ceaseless need for change.

Garrett subsisted on drugs—whatever he could get his hands on— and alcohol. He purchased this diet with the proceeds from petty crime. He sometimes found shelter in the house or apartment of someone he met on the street, but most nights he slept wherever he fell. Garrett's neighborhood was once a thriving and fashionable residential area. But by this time, the large old homes with wraparound porches had been mostly retrofitted into shabby apartments with rows of black mailboxes tacked up near the front door. In the small business district, among the tattoo parlors, coffee houses, and pawnshops, an old but beautiful mainline church sat mostly empty every day but Sunday. On Sunday mornings if the weather was fine, the smooth wooden pews with room for three hundred held twenty or thirty people. The choir room and cavernous Sunday school rooms sat empty.

The denominational leadership was ready to press the last whimper out of this elderly congregation and had decided to close the church. They issued a stay of execution and agreed to wait a few more months; another eager pastor wanted a chance to be the hero. Problem was, her brand of heroics involved change. Instead of keeping the old church and its old ways alive, she wanted the people to join her in creating a new one. Not an easy sell, even for a super hero. But she persisted and led

71

the tiny congregation to a realization: Even though it meant doing something entirely different from what they had done in the past, the people wanted to serve God rather than see their church die. They realized that they needed to do what God needed them to do rather than what they themselves wanted to do. How awesome for a bunch of octogenarians to find this sense of calling!

They partnered with large suburban churches, fixed up the fellowship hall, and started serving sack lunches to the homeless every week. Dirty, addicted, foul-mouthed, foul-smelling people were welcomed into the place where beautiful weddings and baptisms and Christmas pageants had been held for so many years. Garrett started showing up now and then. The pastor invited the dining patrons to show up on Sundays for church. Garrett showed up then, too. Soon he was there every weekday for food and every Sunday for sustenance of a new kind. Garrett, his friends from the street, and the members of this church, found themselves sustained by the gospel messages of grace, love and hope. They glimpsed the possibility of change. They had a vision.

Eighteen months later, Garrett lived substance-free in his own apartment and was employed as director of the fast-growing homeless outreach program at this same church. I'll never forget what he once told me in an interview, as we reflected on the incredible changes God had wrought in his life and in the life of that old church. I hope daily to make it true in my own heart, too: "Now, all I want is to be of maximum service to my God."

Working Toward Vision

Where there is no vision, the people perish
(Proverbs 29:18, KJV).

Different people define vision, like values, in different ways. For the purpose of this discussion, vision is the picture of strived-for change. It's what we *want* to be, what we believe God wants us to be. Your church's culture is *who you are*; your church's vision is *who God wants you to be*. Vision is important because, indeed, without it—without change—we perish.

It's almost a cliché: The only thing we can really count on is change. Our lives, our world, and our churches are dynamic. They change, by necessity.

> Your church's culture is who you are; your church's vision is who God wants you to be.

Your church might have several visions. Some may be lofty while others are relatively simple. Media ministry should be an integral part of achieving whatever visions your church chooses to pursue. Media ministry should help to cast the vision, explain it to the congregation, and inspire the congregation to strive together for this change.

Our church was started by a young, white pastor who was married with children. The church itself mirrored the pastor for the first several years. On any given Sunday, you could look across the congregation and see only Caucasians, and nearly all were between the ages of thirty and forty-five, with children tucked in between. But we knew God's purpose for us meant we should be reaching non- and nominally-religious people who were African-American and Asian-American and twenty-five-year-old singles and seventy-year-old men and women. Today, when you look across the congregation of this same church, you see a much more diverse crowd. There are dark faces and old faces and young adult faces, all tucked in between the thirty-eight-year-old whites. Changing the demographic makeup of a congregation is a practical and pretty simple vision. I'll share a bit about ways media has been part of that vision in the next section of this chapter.

The church Garrett served had a more challenging and far-reaching vision. They needed to change a lot, to move from serving themselves to serving others. If they had a sense of purpose, they applied it only to themselves. They were an insular congregation. They focused their resources on maintenance: they worked hard to do the same things the same ways they'd always done them; they dug in their heels and worked hard to protect their community—shrinking though it was—from outsiders, to maintain their sense of who they were. They built walls high enough so that no one in their community could get out and no one from the outside could get in. Clearly, they would have quietly whimpered and wasted away—like so many other mainline churches—had they not begun to have vision.

Vision like this—broad, sweeping, noble vision—may require a change in purpose. I don't know what happened with Garrett's church; if they had a sense of purpose, they might have simply turned it in a different direction. For instance, if their purpose was "to make disciples of Christ through worship and biblical study," maybe their new vision allowed them to include homeless addicts in the equation for the first time. Or, that vision might have led the congregation to define its purpose altogether, and maybe that occurred for the first time. Vision is God-led change, either incremental or monumental. God makes all things new!

Applying Vision in Your Ministry's Work

It's possible that my own congregation would have moved from homogeny to diversity on its own, without the help of media. Perhaps the community was changing anyway, and the church would have changed right along with it. Perhaps, but I don't think so. At the very least, media helped move the people toward the vision a little faster. In this section, we'll examine ways you can use your media ministry to move your congregation toward whatever vision—or visions—God sets before your church.

Your media ministry is like a mirror, as we explored in the last chapter. Your work reflects your congregation. With the principle of culture, it's like holding up a mirror and saying, "See, this is who we are—we are unique and wonderful and created in God's own image. Let's celebrate!" With the principle of vision, you're holding up a mirror with a different kind of refractive power. Now you're saying, "What if we could be *this*? Wouldn't we be able to serve God better if we were to change in this way? Here's how we can do it, together!" The next section includes examples of ways this principle has been applied in the work of our media ministry at Church of the Resurrection.

Vision Applied in Media at Resurrection

When the church began to see that it was reaching few people of color, people who were young adults, and people over the age of sixty, media was used to reflect a more diverse picture—to help the congregation see themselves a bit differently. I think John Wesley may have originated the idea that we can "do love until you feel it." The same idea applied here. We worked to show the congregation an image that was actually more diverse than reality. We reasoned that if the congregation saw itself differently, maybe it would actually become different. People would tell their twenty-something co-workers about the church's singles program. They'd invite their elderly neighbors to church on Easter Sunday. They'd bring the African-American father of their daughter's classmate to a men's breakfast. So, when the media team does on-camera interviews for stewardship campaign videos, capital campaign videos or sermon illustrations, they try to include African-Americans, Asian-Americans, elderly people, and young people. They also create graphics and other media designed to appeal to a more diverse audience.

Part of how our media ministry applies vision is directly linked to the senior pastor's sermon planning. In May 2005 he preached a series aimed at recent high school graduates. The sermon illustrations included mostly college-age kids. The graphics were designed to reflect that age group's tastes. There were discussions about how to achieve this look without totally alienating the octogenarians every weekend. The media team also created a really cool audio piece, built with original techno-music and snippets from the pastor's sermons, nuggets of wisdom for high school grads to take "out into the world" with them. It was created as a downloadable audio file from the church's website.

In October of the same year, the sermons examined the wisdom of Proverbs. For this series, the media ministry team interviewed only folks over the age of sixty-five—most were well into their seventies. These sermon illustrations held up the congregation's wise sages, and helped the church see itself as more than just a place for young families. The graphics and other visual media for the series echoed the sense of tradition and rootedness and the beauty of age; in fact, the key visual theme for the series was a leaf-covered pathway through the autumn woods, representing the path of wisdom. Beautiful golden and burnished leaves formed the backgrounds for all text during worship. And the interviews were shot at a local arboretum, with the subjects seated along a pathway in the woods, with the pathway stretching beyond and behind them. The crew shot footage of each interviewee walking along the path, standing on a footbridge, or gazing up at the trees and sky. Most of the congregation is still probably between thirty-two and forty-five, married with children. But in six months' time, they saw their church family as something more— twenty-two-year-olds finding their way, and seventy-two-year-olds sharing their way.

Another vision is to revitalize the connection between arts and the church. In centuries past, of course, much of the world's great artistic expressions came out of the church, either naturally or as commissioned works. In the twentieth and twenty-first centuries, however, the arts have been less and less influenced by religion. We'd like to see that change. Church-wide, the staff looks for ways to support and encourage the arts in every aspect of church life. The media ministry, in particular, is a natural arts partner. The creative teams began to incorporate this vision into the design of all graphics, staging elements, and videos. During some seasons this is easy, because the content translates well into a particular artistic form. For instance, there was to be a sermon series covering the major denominations of Christianity. After working through many ideas for a central visual theme, the team settled on stained glass windows. An art student from the local Kansas City Art Institute was hired to create the illustrations. He was given a set of symbols for each denomination—the United Methodist cross and flame, the Pentecostal dove, the Catholic crown and keys, and so forth. He drew a stained glass window panel for each of the eight denominations in the series. He then created one large, classically-arched "window" using the eight individual panels. This young artist's work was then used for the postcard promoting the sermon series to the community, bulletin covers, giant banners for the sanctuary walls, graphics for video illustrations, and graphics for all worship text.

Eventually all large churches realize that they need to recover something that the small church does naturally: beginning to develop small groups, in order to improve individual discipleship and to counteract the disconnectedness that people can experience when they're part of a very large group. Again, media was critical in the effort to pursue this vision at our church. The media ministry team produced a series of videos, which ran approximately every six weeks, promoting the idea of small groups. The first few pieces explained what the groups were, how they functioned, and how to become part of one. Then, after a handful of groups were up and running, the crew began to interview group members about their experience. The pieces showed what it looks like to be in a small group, which was a new concept for many in the congregation: eight to twelve people sitting in someone's living room, talking, sharing, laughing, praying, and breaking bread together. The concept was demystified by the ability to visualize a small group. And the positive testimonies from people who admitted their own initial skepticism helped to defuse the skepticism of many in the congregation. Even when the topic of a video illustration was not focused on small groups, interviewees were asked about that experience in their own lives. So, for instance, for a video or graphics presentation encouraging the congregation to become involved in missions work, an interviewee might describe how his small group did a project together. Or, during the stewardship campaign, an interviewee might discuss how the members of her small group influenced her thinking in this area, helping her to find joy in giving. The same concept applies even if you're not using video; graphics, photo presentations, or audio pieces could achieve the same effect.

This sort of cross-pollination is important; your media communicates the central message—the importance of missions, stewardship, personal faith growth, etc.—and at the same time it lifts up a new image for the congregation. It says, in effect, "See, small groups are how we do things here now. They reach into every part of our church's life and make us stronger, more joyful, and more effective Christians." Only a couple of years after the launch of the church's small-group vision, thousands of people were active participants in home-based Disciple, Alpha, adult Sunday school, or other small groups. Media was critical in this shift, as it held up a new kind of mirror to the congregation and helped the people to see this aspect of Christian life differently.

Vision Applied in Other Church Settings

Demographic changes are common stimulators for visions in churches that seek to draw people of different ages or ethnic backgrounds. Typically, these are churches with traditional worship models, sometimes in rural areas, often with declining numbers of people in the congregation. The most common vision is to see more youth, young adults, or young families become part of the church. The next most common set of visions is aimed at a shift in the purpose or values of the church. Many mainline congregations are striving to move from one focus to another, or to simply broaden their focus to include a new purpose. Examples are churches moving from a focus on missions to a focus on more meaningful worship, or from a focus on community and fellowship to include an emphasis on personal discipleship, or from a teaching-based model to one that promotes evangelism. Whatever vision your church is striving toward, consider these ideas for your media ministry:

Vision on Website

- If your church does not have a website, create one. The pastor should ask the congregation if anyone has any connections to website design and maintenance. This stuff really is like rocket science for many people, myself included. But huge chunks of the population consider this technology about as tricky as working the toaster. Check your local colleges or high schools; there are plenty of teenagers who know how to build and maintain websites! There's bound to be someone in your community who would set up a website for your church and either maintain it or teach your staff to maintain it. It requires a commitment of funds for the server and other technical aspects, but those costs are decreasing all the time. You should consider paying the web administrator, in order to keep the site up and running. What a cool win-win for your church and a high school student! You get your website, and the teenager gets a plum for his very first resume. Your key church staff and volunteers should share responsibility for keeping the site's content current, and for utilizing the site to reach people effectively. You'll need to commit to investing time weekly in order to do this, and a pretty big chunk of time will be required to do the initial training as you get the site off the ground. I don't have the expertise to guide you any further, so check out a few of the many resources available for website development. But for many mainline churches, their website is like a big doorway with a "welcome" sign on it. And young people—from teens to young parents—use this tool daily to get information and to share it. If your church hopes to reach people, a useful website is critical.

RESOURCES FOR WEB DEVELOPMENT:

www.webmonkey.com
www.devx.com/projectcool
www.htmlgoodies.com
www.pageresource.com

Let's assume you've got your website up and running. How do you best use it? Consider the vision, and let it guide you.

- Are you trying to pump up your church's youth department, drawing students to your weekly program for teens? Start there. Make sure the youth department has good visibility on the home page. Add a link for people to find activity schedules. Each month, post slide shows that feature teenagers having a blast together at your church. Design web-based sign-up and registration for youth activities. Develop your own e-vite process, or use one of the many already available on the Internet. E-vites are just what they sound like: e-mail-based invitations. You send a simple e-mail message to your mailing list. Included in the message is an explanation of the event or program you want to promote, and a way to sign up or RSVP. You might also include a link to the church website, where the recipient can find more information about the church and the program. These same ideas translate to other vision objectives; you can use a website to help your church move toward almost any new demographic.

Need a simpler way to help your congregants see themselves differently? Hold up that mirror during worship services! Show them beautiful images of a new vision, and they'll begin to understand why that's who they should be.

Vision in Worship

- First, a couple of simple pointers. Utilize as volunteers the people you're hoping to draw into your church. Get them involved, and they'll invite others. Every ministry of the church should be doing this, but youth and young adults are especially drawn to media ministries, and they're especially good at the work. What a natural way to build toward vision.

- Also, make sure you understand the language of the people you're hoping to attract. Just as you should use and understand the language of your church's unique culture, you must learn to use new languages, too. Watch TV aimed at kids, if they're your target. Look at their magazines. Get on the Internet and surf sites geared toward young families. What colors and images are used? How is information presented? Look for trends and similarities. You'll see a lot of stuff that's inappropriate or even offensive, and you probably won't use it throughout your services, or even every week. But you need to pay attention to the overall design and presentation, and use what you can in the graphics, print, video, and other media work you do at church. When you're attempting to appeal to a new audience, speak their language.

- If you're hoping to attract young families to your congregation, show the young families you've already got. Before the worship services, maybe during the prelude, project slides of that month's activities.

> When you're attempting to appeal to a new audience, speak their language.

Make young families prominent in the sequence; show children at the ice cream social, show young couples in adult Sunday school, and show families working together at the soup kitchen. Help the congregation to see itself differently. Could your pastor encourage congregants to invite young families to church on the first Sunday of each month? They'll be more likely to do this if they have already seen that their church is, indeed, a great place for young families.

- Announcements are another good time to use media to propel your church toward vision. Those announcements should intentionally point people toward the vision, of course. If you're striving to attract more African-Americans, your pastor should be finding ways to invite the congregation to participate in the effort. And the media ministry isn't just a bystander, it's the mouthpiece and the mirror. So, while the pastor invites the congregation to the community's Diversity Prayer Breakfast, show photos reflecting diversity—a couple of children from different ethnic backgrounds playing together at last year's Vacation Bible School, perhaps. Or, before the pastor launches into her explanation and invitation, play a clip on CD from Dr. Martin Luther King Jr.'s "I Have A Dream" speech. (Make sure that you follow copyright laws and have the appropriate permissions.) Those words are so compelling—what a way to grab your congregation's attention. And all you need is a CD player patched through your sound system to do it.

- If the vision you pursue is centered on a shift in purpose or values, use the same techniques described above. Find ways to reflect the new focus whenever possible. Look for ways both subtle and obvious to include the new focus in your communication. When the vision is first identified, your ministry's job is to clearly explain it to the congregation. This will mean many passes at the same information; it should show up in print, on the web, in worship, and anywhere else possible. Design clear and simple graphics to explain the vision during worship, and use these to underscore the pastor's verbal explanation.

> ### A note on using text-based graphics during spoken announcements:
>
> You must rehearse sequences like this with the pastor or whoever is doing the talking over graphics. That person should have a hard copy printout of the slide to be presented, and should have good command of the information. And the text should match nearly word-for-word what is spoken. At the very least, agree on key words and phrases to use both orally and in graphics for each point. Otherwise you'll confuse the congregation; They'll hear one thing while you're asking them to read something else altogether. When you do this, you've violated a big rule in my book! But if you correctly use text-based graphics during spoken announcements, your congregation will be more likely to retain and understand the information.

- After the initial launching stage, your ministry should shift to inspiration mode. Find a few examples of how the change is already happening in your church's life. Is there a Sunday school class that's taking on a mission project together? If your church is seeking to do more in missions, highlight that class during worship. Show photos of their work, or show video clips of it. Interview the people, asking them to explain why they chose to take on such a project, what that decision meant for them as a class, why they think it's important for the church to move in this direction, and how it's changed their own lives as individual Christians.

A Few More Examples

- Be aware that some in your congregation may feel threatened by a push toward vision. It's all about change, and we know what that means: resistance! All of us chafe against change of one kind or another. Expect it here. When you produce media to lead the congregation toward change, do a "preachiness" gut check. Ask someone who's more removed from the project to look at your video, graphics, website, or brochure and adjust their radar to pick up traces of condescension, a self-righteous tone, negativity towards the church as it is today, or anything else that might cause the progress engine to backfire.

- Find ways, through video testimonials, photos, or print pieces, to illustrate for the congregation how this new vision is God-led and important. If the vision doesn't represent a major change in the church's purpose, show the congregation how it's indeed linked to the purpose. The same holds for values—if the vision is just an *expansion* of values, and isn't a major step away from them, then help the congregation see how the two are connected. This continual funneling, staying "on message," remaining constant to one direction is critical for the church. And the media ministry, probably more than any other besides the pastor, is responsible for leading the congregation in this way.

- Finally, in every graphic, video, print piece, web entry, or audio clip, ask yourself if you've communicated the link to the congregant's own personal faith. Is there a way, with a picture, piece of art, or video clip, that you can show how serving in missions will deepen the congregant's faith? Or show them how to share their faith with others and why doing so will bring them closer to Christ? Or show them that Bible study doesn't need to be tedious—they will grow and learn and enjoy a richer faith as a result of it? You have great tools at your disposal, if only a simple graphics program. Use the tools thoughtfully and intentionally, and you'll help people really want to change.

These are just a handful of ideas that I've seen work at churches of all sizes across the country. As leader of your church's media ministry, you're charged with generating other ideas, custom-designed to help your congregation move toward what God wants you to be. Don't leave it to someone else. A few well-chosen photos, a heartfelt video testimony, or a powerful audio clip during worship can be relatively simple to pull off. But consider the impact you can make with those few pictures or a video or a sound clip. Grab your congregation's imagination, appeal to their hearts, and remind them of their love for Christ and for one another. Reflect that new image, and they will change to match it more closely.

> Grab your congregation's imagination, appeal to their hearts, and remind them of their love for Christ and for one another.

Applying Vision in the Formation and Operation of Your Ministry

"We've always done it this way." These words are almost a cliché now for the resistance to change that is such a natural part of our human life. It's like the ludicrous phrase, "Because I said so," which I vowed never to say as a parent. But have I sputtered it out at my kids after grasping futilely for a reasonable response to their "why"? You betcha! That universal fear of change is the first of four things I see getting in the way of media ministry's pursuit of vision. The rest of the list includes complacency, lack of focus on purpose, and a disconnection from God. Let's take a look at them one at a time, with the hope that you may avoid them in your ministry.

Fear of Change

I'm no psychologist, but I can see the fear of change in others and in myself. I'm generally a fairly progress-oriented person who is willing to take risks. But I prefer the changes and risks that are my own idea, or that I see some potential for immediate benefit from. Imposed changes or requested risks are not so much fun. You have the same experience, I'm guessing. We get comfortable with where we are and what we know. And we don't quite trust something that's unknown, even if we believe we should be able to have that trust. Sometimes, that new thing actually seems threatening.

Imagine the little cluster of mostly elderly women at Garrett's church. They'd known each other for decades, thrown baby showers and bridal luncheons for each other, served at church bazaars together, sung in the choir together, and supported one another as they buried their spouses. Through the years, their once-lovely neighborhood had declined depressingly. Who knows all these strange people on the streets nowadays? Why did all the "nice" people head for the suburbs? Who would ever have thought it would come to this—tattoo parlors and homeless drunks just around the corner from the church? And now some young woman pastor has the gall to invite the local street trash into the building and expects the church to feed them lunch every week? I'm sure there must have been one or two folks who were quietly excited by the prospect, but what a tough sell it must have been for most! It would have been nearly unimaginable only a few years earlier. But the vision took hold, and the people moved forward toward this strange new way.

In our media ministries, resistance to change is a big issue: first, from the congregation. We covered this in the chapter on purpose, and the same ideas apply here. People will resist the very existence of a media ministry because, "we've always done it this way, without that stuff in worship, and we don't want to mess things up now!" You'll find it happening within your media ministry itself, soon enough. That's a real mind-blower for me. I've caught myself, staff, and longtime volunteers saying the same things, falling into the same trap: "We've always formatted graphics by category. Why should we change and format them in chronological order now?!" "We've always shot the guitar solos during praise songs. Why should we change and stay on graphics now?!" "The lighting operator always kept the central light on during prayer. Why should we change and bring it down now?!"

The devil I know is better than the one I don't. Even when we intellectually know on some level that change is important and that our resistance to change is not particularly effective, productive, or purposeful, it is often easier to resist change and deal with what we know and understand. This is part of who we are. So know that change will happen, and be ready for it. Have at least one person around who will help you stay away from the trap and will honestly tell you when you're getting too close. Spend time regularly stepping back, reviewing the last few months, praying about how your ministry might move the church forward. Be honest with yourself about your own fears regarding change. And be patient with those around you who are struggling with change, too. Keep holding the image out there, and change will come.

Complacency

There is a law of physics stating that a body in motion is likely to stay in motion and a body at rest is likely to stay at rest. Inertia sets in, in our ministries and in our lives, and we become immobilized. This is related to fear of change. When we give in to that fear and remain unchanged over time, inertia creeps in like rigor mortis. After a while, we feel we couldn't change even if we wanted to. Why does this happen? Why do we allow it? I think that in the church world, and especially in the mainline church world, we have become complacent. I hate to say it, but I wonder now and then if we just don't care enough. Maybe sometimes we're not sure Jesus is worth the trouble. And it seems that sometimes we've been unsure what we really believe, or even *if* we believe at all. It's hard to be passionate about something you don't really believe. For whatever reason, much of the mainline church lost its passion decades ago. (Ah! But it is now awake and can realize what's missing.) If you want to see me blow a gasket, tell me "It's good enough for church" or that "It's *only* for the church." We somehow decided long ago that mediocrity was okay, and that God's church doesn't really require our best efforts. Church work is something to fit in between the other more important pursuits in life, even for ministry "professionals."

If you're reading this book, you'd better feel fired up about media ministry most of the time. You'd better want to get out of bed most days to do this work. Your heart had better race when you start talking about the ways you can use your tools to share the gospel message uniquely in and for your church. We all have our days or weeks or even entire seasons when we're tired or overwhelmed or apathetic or burned out. But this should not be the norm over a year's time.

You need passion for your work perhaps more than others, because you may experience these challenges more often than your counterparts in other ministry areas. Media ministries, as we discussed in earlier chapters, change quickly by nature and are deadline-bound. It's tough sometimes to step back and examine the big picture when you're scrambling fifty-two weeks a year to meet the weekend's deadlines. But important change requires that big-picture view. For many of us, the challenge of meeting the day-to-day demands while planning towards a new vision is overwhelming. We must find a way to step back from that view, and we must look after our own souls, protecting ourselves from the tendency to burn out. We all know the list of things we are to do to take care of our souls, to claim God's peace and calm in our lives. But if you have gone for more than six months feeling overwhelmed, burned out, and complacent, you need to take some time away to reconnect with God's vision for your ministry and your life. You know what that means for you, and only you can make it happen. So, make it happen for yourself. Save your ministry from complacency.

Lack of Focus on Purpose

Earlier, we briefly covered the idea that in some cases vision might point to a change in church purpose. Sometimes our churches *should* change their stated purpose. Sometimes it becomes clear that God needs the church to jump tracks and move in a completely different direction. Often, churches have no real purpose to begin with, but in seeking God's vision, a purpose becomes clear for the first time. I tend to think about it

> Purpose should drive vision, and vision should expand and refine purpose.

the other way around most of the time. Purpose should drive vision. When we focus on a clearly defined and compelling purpose and continually seek God's will for our church, God will refine and hone that purpose for us.

I like to think of it like a set of binoculars; I can see the image of that singer at the opera, but as she moves upstage and downstage, I need to periodically adjust the focus rings, or she goes all blurry. We need God's refocusing as we work on purpose so that we can adjust along the journey to be more effective. Sometimes, as we're successful in one way, God requires us to expand in another way by including some new aspect in our ministry. *Purpose should drive vision, and vision should expand and refine purpose.*

Disconnection from God

It's tempting to conjure up our own vision for the church or for our ministry. Especially if we're not exactly enamored with our church's culture, and would really like to change it lock, stock, and barrel. Let's say you're in an older, tradition-bound church that's railing against the introduction of projector and screens in the sanctuary. Right now, all you can get away with is lyrics for one monthly contemporary service. And even those are as bland as tapioca pudding. You hate the stuff! You could do eye-popping graphics that would make the fogies feel something, for goodness sake. The youth department is finally letting you create some cool stuff for their Wednesday night program, but weekend worship is still stuck. Now, you *could* decide to push hard and cram your wizardry down the congregation's throats, and call it vision. But that wouldn't be right, now would it? What does God want your congregation to be, and how can your ministry be part of that? In this caricaturized example, it's unlikely that God's desire for your congregation is that it suddenly get excited about graphics that appeal to their grandchildren. Most likely, there's something a little more substantive and important in God's vision for you.

Whose Idea Is It, Anyway?

A classic question in this discussion, of course, is how do we know if vision is from God and not just our own idea, driven perhaps by our own will instead of God's? Adam Hamilton leads the staff at Resurrection in a clarifying process to settle this problem, using a series of questions and actions:

- Does the vision line up with the purpose we believe God has given our church?
- Invite God to work through teams of people, and include them in the discernment process. This takes the vision-check out of a solitary person's hands, and allows it to be more thoroughly sifted. Note that team members must know they're allowed to raise doubts and to point out flaws.
- Pray about it. What does the Spirit reveal?
- Daily seek to yield to God's will, to consciously shed your own self-interest and practice walking with God. To the extent we're really able to do this, it deflates the power of our own desires. We experience less fear of giving over to God the big issues of our church and ministry when we've seen God's faithfulness with us on the little issues of everyday life.
- Try something on for size, to see if it fits. Find a way to approach a new vision with a small step, and see how it works, If it does, this might be an indication that this change really is God's will. If not, oh well! You've learned something important, without risking too much.

Finally, know that we may not always be sure that something is God's own will and not just our own idea. But if it's a good idea and serves God's purpose for the church, don't sweat it. It's not wrong or a bad thing, even if you can't firmly declare that God directly gave the vision. Sometimes, God simply blesses a person's vision.

Your pastor should lead the way in the vision-seeking process, but it's also your task. And you know that the only way to know God's will is to seek it. Pray, study, build quiet time into every day, and be held accountable by others for your spiritual life. You know all the right things to do—just do them. It doesn't really matter what you want to do in ministry. My own experience has proven, and I'm guessing yours has too, that we can operate pretty effectively on our own for a while. But when I include God in my life and my work, the unimportant stuff falls away more easily, and I'm more effective in everything I do. If you're doing this work to achieve your own vision of some kind, find a job in the secular world. If you want to be in ministry, find out what God wants you to do. Ask every day, and God will show you.

A Final Word on Vision

Vision can defined in many different ways. A search for vision in the Bible shows us that vision emerges from a variety of sources, illustrating that vision can change. The key is to know that our churches and our media ministries should be changing, too. They should be dynamic!

In the Bible...

- We find the concept of vision as an image or appearance, either real or in a person's mind's eye.
  Genesis 15:1; Numbers 24:4, 16; 1 Samuel 3:15; Matthew 17:9; Luke 24:23; Acts 9:10, 12; Acts 10; Acts 16:9–10
- We find vision as a dream.
  Job 33:15, Daniel, Acts 11
- We find vision as a thought, an idea, or a revelation.
  Psalm 89:19, Isaiah, Ezekiel, Revelation

In these examples and others, God makes God's will known through vision.

Habakkuk teaches us about vision, too. The prophet argues with God over the fate of sin-filled Judah and over God's promise to send the Babylonians to "swallow them up," which confounds Habakkuk. The prophet lays out his arguments one by one with vehement conviction before the Lord. Then, it's as if Habakkuk stops, realizes he's said everything he can say, and takes a deep breath. He continues with a softer voice, I imagine. He writes,

> *I will stand my watch*
> *and station myself on the ramparts;*
> *I will look to see what he will say to me,*
> *and what answer I am to give to this complaint.*
> *(Habakkuk 2:1)*

Sometimes we must climb up high, away from the noise and the deadlines and the workday struggles. We must get ourselves up to a place where we can listen and watch for something that comes from the far distance. That is the only way, sometimes, that we will know what answers to give—to ourselves, to those who we lead, and to those who lead us. So often when we're standing watch on the ramparts, God's will is revealed to us...

> *Then the Lord replied:*
> *"Write down the revelation*
> *and make it plain on tablets*
> *so that a herald may run with it."*
> *(Habakkuk 2:2)*

The Lord replies to us. And then we climb down and tell everyone. We share the vision boldly, making it easy for others to understand. We make the message so easy to see that people can read it even if we're running, holding up the placard as we go.

Do you sense the privilege in that? As the communicators in our churches, we have a wonderful and awesome task. Vision is about change, which can be difficult. But God gives us both the willingness and the capacity to change. That's evident in Garrett and in the people of his church. I can see Garrett standing on the Jerusalem walls, looking out into the distance, listening, murmuring, "All I want is to be of maximum service to you, my God. Whatever that means. Please show me." I hope that you and I will be up there on the ramparts, too.

Questions for Media Ministry Planning

    (1) What is it that God is pressing us to do differently as a church?

    (2) How can we use media to move the congregation toward this new vision?

    (3) Does the vision line up with the purpose we believe God has given our church?

    (4) Have several people been part of the discernment process?

    (5) Are they people who are directly involved on the affected teams?

    (6) Do they feel free to share if they have concerns about the vision?

(7) What do these people think about it?

(8) What does the Spirit reveal about the vision, when we spend time in prayer and meditation?

(9) Are we walking with God, daily turning our lives to God?

(10) Do we fear some aspect of the vision?

(11) Does the change required create a stumbling block for us?

(12) What can we do to hand fear over to God?

(13) How has God proven faithful when we've truly trusted before?

(14) Are we okay to try this on for size? What happens when we do? What do we learn from this that might help us clarify the source of the vision?

CHAPTER FIVE

Excellence

True Story Number One

    People stream into the new building in little rivulets from the parking lots. The narthex is comfortably crowded, and people maneuver their way through the food tables and book displays, looking up and around. Sometimes, they look quite dazed but generally happy. The evening's big session is set to begin in thirty minutes. On the other side of the building, tucked away in the back corner and hidden from the crowd, another scene is playing out.

    Palpable in the video control room is a seething, quiet sense of desperation. One young woman is sprawled on the floor, frantically searching through three large boxes of tapes, checking the labels on each tape against a printed list. Something is missing. Or was it just in that other box? Tears well up in the corner of her eyes as she starts the search again; she looks exhausted. In another corner, two men hunch over the video switcher, punching buttons and twisting knobs, getting in each other's way, bobbing their heads up to check an image in a video monitor. Except that the image never changes. Something isn't working right. Did somebody mess with the settings? Behind sliding glass doors at one end of the room, a young man plugs and unplugs and re-plugs cables on the back of an equipment rack. He is chewing on his lower lip, and his face is slowly turning red. An older man stands nearby, watching helplessly. On the opposite end of the room, two women sit in front of a large computer screen. One juggles a file folder, a cluster of printouts, and a hymnal in her hands, while leaning forward to study the text on-screen. She barks sharply at her partner, "Yes...Yes...No! Change that second line— that's wrong. There's no apostrophe on "its"! Okay. Wait—you didn't save it to the other folder! There...okay, keep going."   The other woman bends over a keyboard, typing and clicking and dragging frantically.

Back in the narthex, amid the cheerful crush of bodies, the music on the loudspeakers fades out under the multitude of voices talking and laughing. In a moment, the first stanza of "Awesome God" plays loudly, and the video monitors high on the walls flip from a scrolling workshop schedule to a shot of the band. People cut their conversations short, glancing up at the screens. They gather up their folders and bags and quickly find trashcans for their cups. The crowd slowly begins to shift toward the large sanctuary doorways. Most of them are smiling with a sense of anticipation. The evening worship session is about to begin.

The production crew snatches their headsets on and scrambles into place. "We're up!" the director says with uneasiness. Their sense of dread is well founded; the session is just short of disastrous. Embarrassing at best. Cues of every variety are missed. Graphics come up at the wrong time, or don't come up at all. Lyrics are out of sequence. The wrong video rolls at one point. The once receptive crowd shuffles out at the end. Some are a bit bewildered. Some are feeling vindicated that, indeed, if something seems too good to be true, it usually is. The production crew halfheartedly tidies the control room and quickly disperses in silence.

True Story Number Two

Two women find their way to a couple of empty seats midway back in the sanctuary. Both are feeling a little nervous as they sit down. The one with short, dark hair is wondering if something, anything, can soothe her tonight. She is worn out with sadness and anger. She has just endured a gut-wrenching betrayal and divorce. Her children are a mess, she's had to take a job she hates to make ends meet, and she will probably still lose her house. But she is at heart a hopeful person, and that flame still flickers somewhere within. The other woman is on staff at this church, hoping that the service will go smoothly. She knows her friend needs to experience Christ's love and his healing, and she wants so deeply for that to begin tonight. There's a pretty decent chance, she thinks; it's a fairly simple service with little opportunity for mistakes.

The two women experience the same worship service, but as soon as it's over, it's clear that they experienced it differently.

The woman on staff practically jumps out of her seat at the end and begins a rapid-fire apology, "Well, that was disappointing—I'm so sorry! Saturday night is kind of rough sometimes, almost like a dress rehearsal. But I can't believe we were late on that audio cue. And the lyrics for one song were all over the place—I'm sure you were totally lost. The sermon was pretty good I thought, except for that graphic that stayed up too long. And we need to do some more training with our camera team, so they can get better shots. Oh well, you caught us on a bad night. I hope you'll come back, maybe on a Sunday. Services are usually more reliable then." The visiting friend deflates slowly during the speech as she shrugs into her coat.

"Actually," she says quietly, *"I thought it was beautiful, the whole thing. And I loved the songs. I didn't notice anything was wrong. I think I needed this…"* Her voice trails off and they walk toward the exit without talking any more. For the first time, the church staffer notices damp streaks down her friend's cheeks, and her wet, red-rimmed eyes.

Worshiping with Excellence

You might be rather offended, I'm guessing, if I preached too much about why it's important that we serve God with excellence. It's a given for most of us—at least we say it is. The concern of this chapter is not *why* excellence is important. Rather, we'll look at *what* excellence is. But just in case you've forgotten, turn to the Bible for evidence of excellence. Consider God's specific instructions through Moses to the Israelites for the building of the tabernacle (Exodus 35–40). This was no lackadaisical request; the orders were specific. Eleven curtains of goat hair for the tent over the tabernacle, each thirty cubits long and four cubits wide. Acacia wood frames, overlaid with gold, fitted and measured exactly, with gold rings at the crossbars. Finely woven fabric of blue, purple and red. A lampstand made of gold, with carefully hammered, almond flower shaped cups. The detailed list goes on and on. This *kind* of detail may not apply in your worship services at all. But God's attention to detail is evident here and throughout the Bible. The Psalms sing, "Shout for joy to God, all the earth! Sing the glory of his name; make his praise glorious" (Psalm 66:1–2), and, "Better is one day in your courts than a thousand elsewhere" (Psalm 84:10). It seems clear to me that God does care about how well we do things, not so much because it's important for us to achieve something, but because of the sacrifice required and the heart that we put into it. For God in this instance, I wonder if the means isn't more important than the end. In any case, I start this chapter with the assumption that excellence is indeed important to God and, therefore, to us.

Excellence is like a strange, otherworldly creature, accompanying me on a long journey. Every time I turn to glance at it, it looks different than the time before. It has seemed boorish, overbearing, exacting, and unrelenting but also lofty, noble, and compelling. What *is* it? What does it require of me? What does it mean to produce worship with excellence? Half the time I want to hop on this creature's back and run with it; half the time I wish it would just go away.

Sad but true are the stories above. Each illustrates a different aspect of the odd beast, excellence. We'll take a closer look at them in this chapter, where we'll examine the principle of excellence. We'll start with an attempt to define excellence in the context of worship production. Then, you'll see how we apply the principle of excellence in our media ministry, with specific examples on the DVD accompanying this book. Next, you'll learn how to apply the principle of excellence in the way you form and operate your media ministry. Finally, you'll review a list of pointed questions. It's my hope that these will become a resource for you, and that over the years they'll help you apply the principle of excellence in your ministry.

An Excellent Journey

If excellence has been my companion on a weird journey, let me relive a few of the curves and hills on that road. In order to spark your thinking about excellence, I'll share with you some of my own experience with it.

Excellence as Attainable

Early on, I felt certain that excellence was something that could be quantified, described, and attained. I could figure it out on my own, list out its various parts, and then see clearly what was needed. From there it was a fairly simple matter of obtaining each thing—a piece of equipment, a volunteer, or a process. I could check items off the list one by one. Certainly there would be occasional adjusting here and there, but I knew that it was possible, with a few years of diligent work, to attain excellence. I soon found out that the "adjusting" was not just occasional; after two years in this ministry, it was obvious that the process of adjusting was continual.

Despite my hopeful ambition, excellence remained nebulous and very big. It was a moving target. Or, if it was standing still, *I* was moving too fast to secure a grip on it.

Excellence as Attainable with Help

Since the ministry was moving so fast and there was so much distance to cover—so much to do each week—I realized what was really necessary to attain excellence was some help. If there were a couple of people alongside me, together we could get our arms around this thing. We squeezed in virtually every project requested. It never occurred to me that it was possible to say, "We don't have the resources to do that." We brought on a handful of part-time staffers. We planned almost nothing ahead of time, and we had almost no sense of process and no real accountability. We did define expectations a bit, setting some rough standards for graphics production and adding deadlines for the submission of song lyrics. We created request forms for others to use when requesting video or other media projects and asked that they be submitted several weeks in advance. But even with the extra bodies, we couldn't achieve what we thought was excellence; we were running around like chickens with our heads cut off.

Excellence as Attainable with Planning

Headless chickens, bumping into things, running over each other. At this point, it seemed that we would have a shot at success if we could just get everybody to stop for a minute and move in the same direction. We started putting energy into planning—schedules, timelines, process maps, worship planning models, and meetings, lots of meetings.

An Excellent Implosion

We were getting closer, but excellence still seemed to elude us. How frustrating. Without revealing too many personal details, I will share that this pursuit of excellence was partly (but not all) the cause of an implosion. Lives with spouses and children started to fracture. Professional ministry careers began to teeter off balance. Staff teams began to fall apart. Avoidable mistakes continued to happen weekly, and improvement seemed to happen hardly at all. Feelings of personal and professional failure ran deep; frustration festered insidiously. We were trying so hard that it felt at times like we were literally

> We continued to miss the mark because we didn't know what it looked like.

killing ourselves, and yet we continued to miss the mark.

And there's the clincher: *We continued to miss the mark because we didn't know what it looked like.*

Excellence Reconstructed

The word *excellence*, like *values* and to some degree *purpose*, is so over-used that it sometimes seems to have lost its meaning. Everybody talks about excellence, waving it around like a flag as if we actually achieve something substantial by merely holding up that flag, pointing to it and saying, "See? We pursue excellence!" But the proof is in the pudding if we walk the walk when the rubber hits the road.

What does *excellence* really mean?

An Excellent Exercise

This section is helpful for any media ministry leader. But it might also be a good one to work through with your media team and/or your pastor and other worship leaders. First, everyone should read the preceding four chapters. Then, work through the exercises here together. If more than four people are participating, you might want to allow a full day for this process. If there are more than eight, you might consider dividing into groups and taking more time. It's most productive to go through the material all at once, rather than a bit at a time over a period of several days or weeks. Momentum is important. You can always go back to review the things you come up with and make changes. But you're more likely to make clear decisions and take lasting action if you plow through this in one fell swoop. It helps to use giant wall-sized Post-it® notes to physically make lists and diagrams as you go. Remember to number and save the notes so that you'll have them for reference later. And guess what? You should go through this exercise every year or so.

What Does Excellence Look Like?

(1) Take a moment now and think about that. In your church, in

your ministry, what does excellence look like? Here are some thought-starters:

- Does excellence mean that there are no misspelled words in any text in your worship service? Does it mean that there are no more than five? Does excellence mean that your worship media is completed a week out, so that your volunteers are not working under pressure as each weekend approaches? Does it mean that you play a congregational news and announcements video each week, or each quarter? Does it mean that the pastor identifies weekly worship as spirit-filled most weeks? Does it mean that the annual pledge campaign always raises 5 percent more than the year before? Or 10 percent? Does it mean that pastors and worship leaders can ad lib, and yet the lyrics and other text will stay on track? Or does it mean that every moment of worship goes as planned 90 percent of the time? Grab a pen and paper, and make an off-the-top-of-your-head list, then set it aside for later.

What Are the PVCV's of Your Church?

(2) Next, go back to chapter 1 and answer the purpose questions. Write out the purpose of your church and of your ministry.

(3) Review chapter 2 and the questions on values. Identify the values that are most important to your church now. List them, describing them as specifically as possible. Describe how they are tied to your purpose.

(4) Move on to culture. What are the words that best describe your church as it really is today? What are the people like? How do they communicate and get information? What sorts of things appeal to them? How do they feel about media in worship, generally? Write down a complete description of your church's culture.

(5) Where do you think God would like you to grow as a congregation? What are the things that should probably change about your church? What are the growing edges, or the places you should be reaching out as a church? Does the pastor articulate a vision? If so, write it down. If not, spend time in reflection and prayer, and see if God reveals anything to you. Write down the vision for your church, if you feel confident about it.

(6) Now, here's a hard part. Look at your lists and notes from each preceding chapter. Summarize the points that you generally agree on for each. Then, try to boil each chapter summary down to no more than three sentences.

What's the Most Important Thing?

- What "floats to the top" from this exercise? What can you identify as the most important thing your ministry should do?

What Are Your Strong and Weak Spots?

(7) Next, you must evaluate your ministry. (See the long-range planning notes in chapter 1 for more ideas on how to do this with your team.)

- What are the strengths and assets available to you? Consider people, facilities, equipment, and the level of commitment in your staff, volunteers, pastors, and congregation. You'll need to leverage every asset, and you can't leverage it if you don't realize you've got it.

- What are the weaknesses or liabilities? Of those weak points, are there ways you can shore them up or fix them quickly? If so, spend the time to write out objectives, and come up with strategies to accomplish them.

- If the weak areas are too entrenched or too complicated or too deep to fix within a couple of months, just mark them down as weaknesses to acknowledge for the time being. You can't fix everything at once, and many things will just have to wait.

What Are You Already Doing Well?

(8) Identify and list the thing (or things) you already do well. What do you currently do with a high degree of success?

- Do you come up with creative ways to integrate media into music? Do you have strong graphic design skills on the team? Is your video editor a wizard? Do you have a volunteer or staffer who works really well with the pastor? Is there a strong writer on your team? Do you have administrative and organizational skills? Do you have someone who can troubleshoot and correct just about any technical problem?

Make a Most Important Plan

(9) Now consider the list of available assets you made earlier. How might you combine those with the things you already do well, to achieve that most important thing? Look at your lists. What trends do you see? Where is there overlap? What are the gaps? Use all this information to formulate a plan.

> Success = (1) You did what you planned the way you planned it, and (2) What you planned had the effect you intended. (Tip: Use these as your criteria for weekly evaluation.)

Consider this hypothetical case study:

Let's say you've identified the most important thing you should do as providing mood-setting graphics to facilitate praise and worship for your young adult group's weekly worship service. The graphic designs need to be strong and innovative but simple. And you'll need a lot of variety, because your church does twenty minutes' worth of praise and worship at this service. You see a way to make this happen:

- You have a young volunteer, Sue, with great Internet research skills, computer operation skills, and an eye for what works in your church setting. She'll be responsible for finding great images. Sue learned most of her computer skills from her teenage son, Brian, who is a self-confessed geek.

- Another volunteer, Ted, is a musician and artist. He knows how to use Adobe Photoshop and can manipulate images to create innovative backgrounds. Ted is fun to work with, and people like him even though he is scattered and unorganized.

- Your church is fortunate to have Marty, an IT specialist at a local firm. She has helped get the church website up and running and has advised the church council on IT issues. You call her and invite her to do a couple of training sessions with Sue, Ted, and Brian. She'll show Sue and Ted how to organize the computer files, store backgrounds on the church's server, and download graphics into the worship presentation software sequence each week. She agrees to meet with Brian for an hour on the first Saturday of each month to troubleshoot and maintain the system. He becomes her apprentice. She's able to back off on the massive time commitment she's had while getting the website up, but is still able to serve the church. And her efforts are multiplied as she equips Brian.

- You have good organizational and leadership skills. You make a recruiting plan and work with the church's Lay Leadership Team. They are very effective at helping members get plugged into service in the church, but until this point you haven't really been able to capitalize on their efforts. Now you're ready. You create a simple team structure comprised of three teams: Design Team, Operation Team, and Tech Team. The Lay Leadership Team will help you recruit three people for each team.

- You'll work with Sue and Ted to develop their leadership skills. Ted will lead the design team in creating great images each week. Sue will lead the operation team in formatting and sequencing the images, and they'll run the system during worship. Brian leads the Tech Team and is joined by a couple of grown-ups. They look to him for his expertise, and they provide maturity and wisdom. Together, this team makes sure the system is running smoothly during worship each week.

Setting Boundaries

As part of this process, you'll need to identify the things you're willing to let go of, at least for now. There must be clear boundaries around what your ministry will and won't do. Probably nothing will kill a media ministry faster than lack of boundaries—especially if it is run by volunteers. Once a media ministry is up and running, people see the power and effectiveness of the tool and want to use it in their ministries. Naturally! I have seen and heard this story over and over, in churches of all sizes. People who do this work, for pay or for free, love it and want to share it. But without restriction, these people will burn out. So, it's important to understand what's most important, what your ministry can do well, and what your current limitations are.

An example: If you have a real gap in video editing, table video production for a while, until you're able to find a way to fill that gap. Concentrate instead on animated graphic backgrounds. Or, if your technical team is stretched too thin to manage the systems every week, scale back to bi-weekly or monthly media in worship. Chances are that the congregation will begin to miss it on the "off" weeks, and your next recruiting effort may yield good fruit.

> It's important to understand what's most important, what your ministry can do well, and what your current limitations are.

Another case in point: At Resurrection, our graphics were pitifully weak for many years. When we started the ministry, we had strength in writing and producing testimony-based videos. That was it. So we capitalized on that strength and used it to help do what was most important. For us, it meant weekly video sermon illustrations. Later, we gained equipment assets, and combined those with live production skills to develop successful image magnification in worship. Other churches were producing beautiful graphics, but we were still doing the most basic sans-serif-text-on-blue-background, with the occasional zippy addition of (yuck!) clip art. It wasn't until six years into media ministry that we even started attempting to beef up the quality of our graphics. And then it was only because a volunteer and a part-time staffer showed interest and potential. They did some training, spent hours playing around in Photoshop, and went on to develop graphics stylebooks and procedures. They recruited and trained our first teams of graphics volunteers.

Defining Excellence for Your Ministry

This is important. I hope that you've now identified what's most important for your ministry to do and that you see how to use what you've got in order to do it. At the same time, you will almost certainly need to identify what things you will *not* do, because they are *not* the important thing, and because you cannot do them well at this time. These two things together begin to define excellence for your ministry.

Point to remember #1: Do what is most important, in a way that you can do it successfully.

Point to remember #2: You must define what excellence looks like in your own church setting, for your own ministry.

The work you've done up to this point—clarifying the purpose, values, culture, and vision of your church and your ministry, as well as identifying the most important thing you can do successfully—should give you a new sense of understanding. It may take a while to sink in and digest. But as the ministry's leader, it is your responsibility to define excellence. If you chase after another person or church's idea of excellence, you will always be chasing. Your task now is to put *your own ideas about excellence* down on paper or in some way that you can share them. You'll need buy-in from pastors and others. Once again, you might find yourself leading other volunteers or staff in a new direction as you invite them to participate with you in this quest.

Make the Sale

An effective proposal or ministry statement can go a long way in gaining buy-in from others. Here are some things to remember when you're trying to make the sale:

- Write it down in a neat, concise, easy-to-read document.
- Be specific, giving details to support each point.
- Explain the "before" and "after" picture, so that the reader has a frame of reference for what you're doing now and how that will change under the new policy.
- List the resources required to do what you're proposing.
- For resources that you need but don't currently have, include a summary of how you plan to obtain them.
- Include a list of all costs associated with the proposal.
- Explain, using specific examples, what you'll be able to do under this new policy that you can't do now.
- Explain, using specific examples, how the proposal is linked to purpose, values, or vision.
- If writing proposals is not your strong suit, recruit someone else to do it for you.

Excellence as Perfection

A wise-beyond-his-years manager told me something near the end of my "Excellent Implosion" period that I hope will offer you encouragement. As I worked to begin reconstructing the ministry, I met with him to share my ideas and struggles. At one meeting, I enthusiastically explained my plans for new structure and new standards. I was certain these strategies would turn everything around and set us back on the right road (to excellence). At one point I said, "When we get these new strategies in place, we will do everything we can to make worship the best it can be." He cut me off, and asked me to stop and think about what I'd just said. "Can you really do that?" he asked. "Is that really what the church *needs* you to do—'everything you can, to make it the best it can be?'" I realized in an instant that I was talking the old talk, which would inevitably lead to what I'd just come from—implosion. That sort of "Everything You Can…Best It Can Be" definition of excellence is unattainable and self-destructive.

But, we might ask, "God deserves nothing less than as close to perfect as we can get, right?" That's right, but not exactly. When we equate excellence with perfection, we think too highly of our own capabilities and too little of God's. As we go through the journey trying to serve the Lord with excellence, we must carefully and prayerfully define it.

> When we equate excellence with perfection, we think too highly of our own capabilities and too little of God's.

From step one of the "Excellent Exercise" at the beginning of this section, take out your list of the ways you define excellence for your ministry. Spend time in prayer, asking the Holy Spirit to guide you and to reveal the things that really should define excellence for you.

Excellent Execution

Excellence applies to two broad categories: (1) what you do, and (2) how you do it. Purpose, values, culture, and vision are all about the *what*. Especially if you've worked through the exercises above, you should understand excellence as it relates to your unique *what*. Execution is the *how*.

Remember, we're not talking about perfection here. We're talking about intentionally setting the standards for execution that make sense for your own ministry and your own church. What follows is a list of examples, ideas, things to try, and tips related to the excellent execution of media in worship.

A Moving Target

You'll remember that early on in ministry I naively thought I could capture the things that make up excellence in one good list, check items off as I accomplished or obtained them, and be done with it. Finito. Excellence achieved.

I have since learned that excellence is a moving target. It should be defined at least yearly. It should be defined for all the different aspects of your ministry. And it should be defined specifically for projects that involve other ministries or that are unique in some other way.

The Three-Gate Rule

For all graphics or videos—for any media you produce—establish a minimum of three mistake-catching "gates." Three different opportunities for someone to catch a mistake before it goes up in worship. Example: Song lyrics should be read by the person who initially types them (gate 1), then proofed by the person who formats the sequence for worship playback (gate 2), and finally, a producer or someone similar should proof the lyrics by running through the sequence (gate 3). Try walking through your production processes, and see if you have three gates up to prevent mistakes at each important step.

People as Priority

Paid and unpaid servants are the single most important factor in your ministry's capacity to achieve excellence. Not equipment, not facilities, not funding. Recruiting, training, spiritual nurturing, fellowship, and recognition are each critical. I made at least three mistakes before I realized that the participants are the key to an excellent media ministry:

(1) Early on, I didn't understand that volunteers would be/could be/should be critically involved in the execution of media in worship.

(2) At times, I have not defined clearly enough the expectations for volunteer roles, nor have I clarified the boundaries between staff responsibility and volunteer responsibility.

(3) At times, I have put people in positions—both staff and volunteers—where I suspected they might not be able to succeed, usually with predictably poor results.

Mistake #1

I tried for too long to do most of the work myself. I wrote, produced, directed, and edited most material myself for the first couple of years. One of the pivotal moments in our ministry came one Sunday night when a particularly wise volunteer, who served as Technical Director on a worship crew, stopped me in the hallway after worship. He approached me carefully, and I could tell as he began to speak that he was trying not to offend or hurt me. But I needed to hear what he said. I'd just finished directing the sixth and final worship service of the weekend, as I did every weekend at that time. "You're a good director," he said, "But you're going to restrict the growth of the ministry if you continue to direct each service and do all the other critical work yourself. Other people could learn how to do this, if you would teach them. You're already past your own capacity, and unless you turn some things over to volunteers and staff, you'll burn yourself out, you won't have anyone to share the load, and you'll keep your own ministry from growing." This man was so right. Within a few months, I had begun to hand off pieces of the work, and was amazed at the results. Watch the people who serve in ministry with you closely—keep an eye on anyone who seems to hang out with the crew, in fact, if they're hanging out with the sound person or team, they're probably interested!

- Look for potential: calmness, directness, carefulness, thoughtfulness, an eye for good framing, strong graphic design, and technical skill. Look for whatever are the most important characteristics for your ministry.

- Look for commitment to, and understanding of, your church's purpose, values, culture, and vision—look for people who "get it" and who are completely on board with the direction your ministry and church are going.

- Look for teachability, that willingness to come under another's direction. Look for people who are not just willing to learn a new skill but who are willing to do things your way. This may seem crass or harsh, but it's critical. Your work is exacting, stressful, and creative. And, let's face it, everyone in the congregation sees or hears your every mistake each weekend. By contrast, if a few choir members hit wrong notes or botch a rhythm, most congregants will not know. But the choir director has every right to expect that those choristers follow his cues, learn their music, and sing it his way. It's his or her role as director to lead everyone in expressing that music. Likewise, it's your role to lead those who serve in your ministry. And we can't lead those who refuse to follow.

• Finally, look for people who are committed to serving Christ. Your ministry will naturally attract people who are interested in the cool toys or the rush of live production. That's okay, but the primary driver must be love for the Lord and a sincere and humble desire to serve in whatever way they're needed.

When you see people with these attributes, pour into them. Develop, train, tutor, and mentor them. If you can't, then make certain a volunteer leader or another staffer is doing this. Some of our most brilliant and devoted staff started out as volunteers with little skill or experience but lots of potential.

Mistake #2

Volunteers are, for most churches, the only way to run a media ministry. We could never afford to pay for all the professional staff it would take to run every event, produce every video or print piece, and create all the graphics and other media. Beyond that, we wouldn't want to! Part of the beauty of your ministry is seeing people serve Christ in such a unique way. For many, it is *the* way they can serve that really uses their gifts and feels right. Your ministry becomes, then, a blessing for the volunteers, a blessing to the church, and a blessing to the Lord. However, it's your responsibility to place very clear parameters around those volunteer tasks. It's tempting to hand over too much, especially when you're overwhelmed as it is. But you must explain and put in writing the boundaries for volunteers and staff. Here's why:

• For important or wide-reaching projects, including weekly worship, staff should always be directly involved, supervising and making major decisions. Typically, staff are at the weekday meetings where planning occurs.

  ◦ Here's a rule of thumb: if staff are the primary planners of an event or project, then staff should be the primary producers of it and should be responsible for execution. Otherwise, you're putting volunteers in the position of working in a direction that may not be in sync with the rest of the project. This creates a lot of problems for you, for the church, and for the volunteer.

- It's our natural tendency to be territorial. When we settle into a spot where we feel valued and important and capable, we like to drive stakes into the ground and start putting up fences to mark our spot. I've heard the same complaint from our colleagues around the country, in large and small churches: "I have a volunteer who is trying to run the system all by himself, and it's gotten out of control. He won't make the changes I ask him to make, won't do things the way I tell him we need to, won't let anybody new in, and hoards all the work himself, even though it's way too much for any one person to handle." Sound familiar? Setting clear expectations and parameters will help combat this problem and others. (One of your parameters should be that people move around—that team leaders train new people for their position every so often, and then move to another spot.) If you need to make changes and have an already-entrenched volunteer, put the changes in writing—a covenant is a good tool—and explain to *all* the volunteers that this is a new expectation for everyone, and that you'll hold them accountable to it. This is a great exit-with-dignity strategy for entrenched volunteers. The covenant or policy statement spells out your boundaries, and gives folks a chance to re-evaluate their service with a ready-made reason to bow out if necessary. Just make sure you do hold people accountable.

- Burnout is rampant in media ministries, in part because we don't set clear parameters. Even volunteers who are not entrenched will burn out because of the sheer amount of work and stress in this ministry. And because the work is so specialized, we often lack qualified volunteers; the committed ones see the need and jump in even when they're already exhausted. Place limits on how many hours per week your volunteers can serve, or how many projects in succession. Find ways to be more efficient, and hire staff to do a job when it gets to the point of consistently taxing volunteers beyond capacity.

- If we as staff hand over the wrong kinds of tasks—particularly the decision-making and supervisory tasks—we are not doing what the congregation pays us to do. The staff-parish committee, church council, pastor and others count on us to understand the policies and priorities of the church and to run our ministries accordingly. It's our responsibility, and our job on the line, if things don't go as planned.

Mistake #3

If you're in a small or medium-sized church, you're probably a volunteer leading the media ministry. If you're paid staff, you're likely the only one. And you might be serving as worship leader or youth director or associate pastor or IT director at the same time! If your prayers are answered, or a miracle occurs, and you're given the green light to hire staff, you will rejoice. For a little while. Then you'll realize that it can be tough to find people who are committed to Christian ministry, have the skills you need, and will work for what the church can pay. You may begin talking yourself into bringing on people who clearly are not a match for the job, out of desperation. Take your time. Get permission to drop chunks of your workload, if necessary, until you find the right person. Or divvy the job up and hand off pieces to other staff or volunteers, until you find the right person. If your gut tells you that someone will struggle to fit in on your team, will chafe against your leadership, or will not be able to do the work, keep looking.

Paid and unpaid servants are the single most important asset for your ministry. Serve with volunteers, set clear expectations for everyone, and hire people you're excited to have on your team.

Excellence Per Project

You'll define excellence not only for your overall ministry's work, but also for individual projects. Excellence may look different for one project than it does for another. You must clearly define excellence for the people who are working on the project and for the people who will use the project. In biz-buzz, they call this "managing expectations." So, before you set to work on a video or graphics or web design, spell out your expectations. How much time will you have to devote to it? How many revisions will you be able to make, and what is the process for those? What are the deadlines you need others to meet in order to get the project finished? What are the resources available, and what resources do you still need? Define what you're aiming for before you begin, and share it with the project stakeholders—anyone who will contribute to or be impacted by the project. This is a good habit to develop while your ministry is small and fairly simple. It becomes critical when your ministry grows, as you have multiple people contributing to and feeling the impact of your ministry's work.

Buy or Rent the Best Gear You Can Afford

Churches often take hand-me-downs or discards. Once again, we should identify the important things for our media ministry to do, and then put resources there. A shoddy screen, a dim projector, an old camera, a discarded DVD player, and an outdated computer graphics system might seem to constitute a "full-fledged media ministry," which you may feel pressure or the desire to have. But most churches would be better off with less equipment, of better quality. You may need to choose to use video monthly rather than weekly, and rent equipment until you can purchase it. Especially in older churches where there is resistance to begin with, bad gear will just prove the resister's point—it won't be reliable and won't add to the quality of worship.

Buy or rent the gear you need to do the important things for your ministry. Expect to build slowly, not all at once. Use the best quality equipment you can afford.

> Expect to build slowly, not all at once.

Remember to Breathe

It drives my kids crazy now, but when they get hurt or get a vaccination or some other painful event occurs, my first response is usually to tell them to remember to breathe. I started this when they would get overwhelmed as toddlers, crying until they couldn't even suck in a breath. Sitting in the skybox or control room, watching worship services as the person responsible for excellent execution has at times been so painful that a stubbed toe or tetanus shot would have been lovely in comparison. If I ever cried, it was only slightly.

But for several years, until staffing additions meant I could pass this task on to someone else, I came home every Sunday night feeling battered and burdened. I would sit through an hour's service and see a hundred large and small mistakes, feeling frustration churning hotter and faster. Nothing is ever finished (see more on this in the last section, below), and nothing is ever good enough. We are people, not robots, running equipment in a complicated matrix, with infinite variables. Mistakes happen. But they can drive you crazy. Your reaction, especially if you are the leader of the ministry, is key and will impact everyone else around you.

- Train yourself and your teams to move on through mistakes. Don't stop to analyze the problem at the time; recover and go on. Otherwise, you're likely to set off a domino effect of problems for the rest of the service. As leader, your job is to say, "It's okay, we'll look at that later. Let's keep moving…Good job!"

- Have a process to record the mistake somehow—maybe a volunteer whose task is simply to make notes about what happens during the service, including as much info as possible to flesh out the evaluation later. Include both the good and the bad.

- As soon as the service is over, privately pull aside the persons involved in any major, service-disrupting mistakes. First, encourage them about what they did well. Then, remember that they probably feel awful about the mistake already. Your task is not to make sure they feel awful, or that they feel really, really awful enough. Your task is to encourage, help them discover what happened and why, and facilitate an agreement on how together you'll prevent the same mistake in the future.

- What's not acceptable is explosion or blaming. This damages your credibility, fractures the team, creates an atmosphere of distrust, and, most importantly, hurts people. If you're prone to angry outbursts, tantrums, or bitter language, find a way to deal with the inevitable frustration without resorting to those behaviors. This should go without saying, particularly in the church, but there are lots of us in production, music, and related ministries who are challenged with these issues. We all are sinners who fall short of the glory God desires for us. For some, sin is more easily concealed from people. For those who struggle in the way I've described, extra effort is required to keep from destroying people and ministry.

- Remember that worship is not about you or your team or your ministry's ability to look good on any given Sunday. Worship would happen if every piece of equipment shut down. Think happy thoughts, and know you'll attack the problems on Monday. Remember to breathe!

An Almost-sacred Rule: Media Should Never Distract from Worship!

Media should never steal the congregation's attention away from the main focus of worship. It should never make them disengage. They should never wonder, "What's happening?" "Why are those words different than what the singer is singing?" "What is that image supposed to mean?" This is at the very heart of what we do, and it's what makes us lay awake at night, isn't it? We work alongside musicians and pastors and liturgists to create worship that's engaging (or whatever you define as the objective of your service), and we pour time, energy, and prayer into each week. We arrive at the weekend anticipating the movement of the Holy Spirit in our midst. But the congregation can be yanked out of the worship experience in a moment. This is the gut-wrencher for me. Some thoughts:

- Know that this will be your struggle for as long as you're in media ministry. You will strive to improve, put new strategies in place, train volunteers more effectively, hire staff, beef up communication, and do lots of other things to reduce mistakes in execution. But at the same time, you'll be trying new things and adding more complexity, which results in a more challenging event. So every week you'll have to sit across the table from the pastor and explain that week's batch of gaffes. Think of it this way: If it were easy, you'd be bored.

- Know that often a mistake that seems to belong on your rap sheet actually belongs somewhere else. Communication between music and media departments is a typically difficult area. Your best tactic is to build strong and positive partnerships with your colleagues in music, clergy, and drama or with whoever else serves alongside you in planning worship. This team should be small and close, and it should be built on trust. Especially if this is not the case, know that you'll be tagged with penalties unfairly. If lyrics are off, everyone assumes the graphics person goofed, and so on. You are the obvious target for blame, warranted or not. Avoid the urge to finger-point. The backstory is usually too complicated to explain, and only you will really understand the role others have in execution problems; you'll be perceived as making excuses. Instead, find ways to close communication gaps, and develop processes that will eliminate avoidable mistakes. You must take the initiative here.

- Usually, media is not the focus of worship. Rather, it points the congregation toward the focus. It illuminates or illustrates. It's not the central point itself; it only supports the point. There are exceptions to this, but it's important not to get caught up in the fun stuff you can do, if it's at the expense of focusing the congregation on each moment in worship. Too often, a cool experiment can derail worship.

- Sometimes, you will create something that, in the end, doesn't work. When this happens, don't use it. Replace a clunker graphic with an old standby. Drop the video from worship. Yes, you and your team will have spent time on something that ended up being trashed. But it's not a waste of time. Flops are part of the creative process. They should be rare, of course, or you've got a problem. But if it's clear that an element may cause a disconnect for the congregation, you must drop it.

> But if it's clear that an element may cause a disconnect for the congregation, you must drop it.

Media in worship should never distract or cause a disconnect for the congregation! "Never" is, of course, too much to live up to, but it should be our target.

Applying Excellence in the Formation and Operation of Your Ministry

Let's assume you've done all the work suggested in this chapter thus far. You know what's most important and what you can do well, you've defined what excellence looks like for your ministry at this point in time, you understand that perfection is *not* your goal, and you're continually refining your execution. Other traps and snares may be hiding along your path; following are some that I've encountered, shared so that you may be able to avoid them.

Lack of understanding of the ministry leader's strengths and weaknesses

If you are the ministry leader, it's important for you especially to understand the hard, cold reality of what you're able to do and what you're not. The leader, like everyone else, brings capabilities to the job, but there are inevitably gaps in what that person can do well. It helps me to look at the team as a puzzle or a picture, or to make a sort of chart showing strengths and weaknesses. Try this exercise, even if only in your head. (1) Write or draw out the characteristics and capabilities that are necessary in your ministry to achieve whatever you've defined as excellence. (2) Next, write or draw out the characteristics you personally possess. (3) Then, do the same with others on your team. (4) What of the first list—the required characteristics and capabilities—do you have covered in your team? Are you lopsided, with lots of technical depth but too little leadership skill? Or do you have mature Christian leaders with very little creativity? Or is the team very creative but lacking in time and resource management skills? Again, we see that it's people, not equipment, that are critical to doing media with excellence. But we must have at least a mostly-complete picture or puzzle, with the critical characteristics and capabilities covered, in order to achieve what we set out to achieve. As you build your ministry, recruit people for volunteer and staff positions that will complete the picture.

Lack of Commitment

The work you do requires an extraordinary commitment of time and energy. I once worked with someone who regularly pointed out that "yours is the most expensive ministry in the church." He was thinking of financial expense, but I believe the greatest cost is in people's time and energy. You already know that it takes hours to produce a graphics sequence, and even longer—days or weeks—to produce a video. People who have never actually done this work, which is probably nearly everyone you work with, have a hard time understanding why it could possibly take so long. Add to that the time required for planning and thinking, as I've outlined in this book, and your commitment is substantial. Then we must account for the technical glitches, equipment failures, and unexpected repairs that seem to be a constant drain, especially with older equipment. There are also the surprise projects that must get wedged into the workload. And then, of course, there are the regular meetings, budgets, and other tasks required in your job. You will likely work every weekend, at least until your ministry has grown to the point that you can hand that off to others. Similarly, you will likely work many evenings—for meetings with volunteers, for music and worship rehearsals, and just to get the week's product finished. If you have a spouse and/or children, they will feel the impact of your absence. You'll be gone for most of Advent and Christmas, and most of Holy Week and Easter.

Does that seem like a dreadful list? Maybe. But it's also the reality of media ministry leadership—the downside that you need to face squarely. Every downside has an upside, however. What are the things that you love about this ministry? Is it enough to get you out of bed every morning?

If you were suddenly unable to do this work, would you miss it? Media ministry is incredibly demanding in many ways and will likely impact virtually every aspect of your life. Hardly anyone will understand your work or its demands, including your colleagues at the church. Your family and friends will bear a great deal of the impact. If, knowing all this, you love what you do and take great joy in it, if you're propelled out of bed each day in order to get to it, and if you can't imagine doing anything else, then you're in the right place. You're committed. The downside is outweighed by the upside.

For me, the impact on my family has been the biggest challenge. But even they have seemed to share my commitment all along. I saw that pretty clearly when our middle daughter was four years old. I was tucking the kids into bed on December 23rd. I explained to them that the next day I would be gone from lunchtime on, but that I'd see them when they and Daddy came to church and that I'd be home when they woke up on Christmas morning. One of the kids whimpered a little and said, "You mean you'll be gone that whole time on Christmas Eve?" But before I could reply, Olivia said, "It's okay Mommy. We know that you have to be there to help other people find out about Jesus, because they don't know about him like we do."

Lack of Flexibility

Media ministry moves fast. You've probably gotten that idea by now. Everything seems to be constantly changing. You're never finished with anything. Something always seems to need repair or replacement. You make one set of improvements and then see a whole new cluster of trouble spots. You work with people, so there are continual human issues facing you. Schedules are drawn up, color-coded, and distributed to the team, but then a week later they're out of date. You're working to finish projects for the weekend every Friday or Saturday. You live with the nagging feeling that if some catastrophe were to occur—an irretrievable computer crash, for instance—you would be sunk, because you're working so close to the edge. Remember the scene from the movie *Broadcast News* where Joan Cusack's character literally runs a videotape from the edit bay to the control room just in time for it to play on the air? Media ministry often works like that. And it doesn't ease up entirely. In fact, if you're effective in your work—if you're doing ministry with excellence—your ministry and probably your church will grow. And the fast track will notch up in velocity bit by bit, every year. You need to be okay with that, and you need to be okay with the fact that it won't change much.

Story One and Story Two

Remember True Story One and True Story Two, at the beginning of this chapter? They're instructive for us as we consider how to run our ministries with excellence, and they illustrate what I think are the two most important things to remember from this chapter:

(1) Don't try to do too much.

(2) Remember how God works.

In True Story One, we see a media ministry gone awry. Chaos, frustration, anger, ineffectiveness, mistakes—this is not what you want to see in your ministry, is it? That event was a huge missed opportunity for us. We had more than a thousand people gathered in our sanctuary, anticipating that something meaningful and excellent would move them. Instead, we distracted and confused them. The reason? We overreached, trying to do too much. There were too many cameras to keep track of, too many videotapes for playback, too little training for the crew, and too many crossed wires in the pre-production stage. The right hand had no clue that there even *was* a left hand. Staff were too overwhelmed to supervise properly, and volunteers were trying to do more than they were able. Deadlines were not met by others on church staff. Graphics input piled up on the final two days. Last-minute changes arrived just minutes before "air" time. Each of these problems could have been avoided. But we had not defined excellence for the event, nor had we evaluated our resources. It hurts to admit this, but we had just moved into a new building and were eager to show it off. We thought too little and promised too much. In the end, we failed. That failure affected our ministry in myriad ways, for more than a year. If I could urge you to retain one thing regarding excellence, it would be that you must avoid the temptation to do too much, too soon. In the end, excellence in church media has very little to do with making an impression or doing impressive work. It is much more about defining specifically how your ministry will serve your church's purpose, values, culture, and vision.

> In the end, excellence in church media has very little to do with making an impression or doing impressive work. It is much more about defining specifically how your ministry will serve your church's purpose, values, culture, and vision.

In True Story Number Two, we see two women experience the same hour of worship very differently. For the media team staffer, it was a disappointment. For her hurting friend, it was an hour of sacred time reconnecting with the healing Christ. True Story Two illustrates that after all our efforts to define excellence for our ministry so that it will serve the church well, we must remember that God will work in the church regardless of what we do or how well we do it. The details that drive us to distraction are often unseen by others. It's important for us to work on those details, but too often we discount God's ability to work *through* them. People have worshiped through the centuries without video screens, projected lyrics, beautiful pictures, and theatrical lighting. To state the painfully obvious, God is present even when those things are not.

This, I think, is where we get perfection and excellence dangerously confused. When video, graphics, lighting, or sound are off and we can't seem to produce what we see in our mind's eye or what we hear in our heads, we can become indignant, even angry. "I can't help it, I'm a perfectionist." We say that as if it's equivalent to saying, "I'm trying to do this with excellence." But the two are different. I can produce an excellent video if excellence is something I've defined intentionally for my ministry and for that project. "Perfect" is what I see in my mind's eye or hear in my head. I believe God put those images and sounds there for me, but I know I will never be able to produce a perfect video. For me to say "I'm a perfectionist," and for me to believe somehow that I *can* do something perfect is egocentric and ignores God's role.

One of the wisest people I know pointed out this rather painful concept for me. He told me to give up "the last 15 percent." That 15 percent is the final stage of a project—when it's finished, but I continue to refine. The hours, energy, and angst I expend when trying to polish a project at that point are wasted most of the time. I'm the only one who would notice much of the difference. I've started to ask this question: Will these further refinements increase the impact on the congregation, or will they simply make me feel better about the project myself? If the impact will increase, I'll keep working. If not, I know I've reached the 15 percent point and should wrap it up.

And here is the difference for me between excellence and perfection: You and I can do media in our churches with excellence. But that last 15 percent belongs to God; God fills the gap and delivers perfection. The egocentric staffer in True Story Number Two is me; I'm ashamed to admit it. The worship service in that story was a little short of excellent, as we've defined it, but not far short. I took my friend to church that night hoping to show her "perfect" and was disappointed when I thought that didn't happen. But, in fact, it did happen. God was present, as God always is. And perfect God gave my friend exactly what she needed. God makes our excellent perfect.

Questions for Media Ministry Planning

(1) How do we currently define excellence? Is that realistic?

(2) What is most important for our ministry to do related to purpose, values, culture and vision?

(3) What are the resources and assets available to us?

(4) What are the weaknesses and liabilities of our ministry?

(5) What are the things we do really well?

(6) How might we combine the things we already do well and the assets available to us to serve the important thing?

(7) What do we need to let go of?

(8) What is our new definition of excellence—for the ministry, and for each project?

(9) Do we equate excellence with perfection?

(10) What are the ways we could use volunteers more?

(11) Have we clearly defined our expectations for staff and volunteers?

(12) Do we have the right people on our team?

(13) When considering a specific media-based element for worship, will it likely cause a disconnect for the congregation? Will it distract their attention from what's important at that moment in worship?

(14) As ministry leaders, do we understand our own strengths and weaknesses?

(15) Are we able to make the necessary commitment?

(16) Are we charged up (or beaten down) by the pace of media production?

(17) When planning a project or event, are we overreaching? Do we feel anxious about our ability to pull it off within our own definition of excellence?

(18) Are we aware of the way God works in our ministry?

—

CHAPTER SIX
Meaning

The tall, lanky man sits next to his well-dressed wife as the worship service begins. He crosses his arms over his chest and settles into his seat, silently fuming. His golfing opportunity missed, he resigns himself to get through the next hour without noticeably falling asleep. She, on the other hand, sits upright and attentive. She glances over at him hopefully during the opening announcements; he stares straight ahead, expressionless.

An organ begins to play. The choir and small orchestra are suddenly lit up, and everyone rises to their feet. As he begrudgingly stands, the man notices words appearing on a big screen at the front of the sanctuary. The people all look up and begin to sing together. He watches and listens; his wife joins in rather tentatively. It creeps up on him, a feeling that he has had this experience before, that he has heard this sound and these words before. A mighty fortress is our God, a bulwark never failing; our helper he amid the flood of mortal ills prevailing. He stands very still, and his breathing becomes shallow. He is trying to figure it out. What is this feeling? It washes over him like a wave: He is ten years old, standing in church next to his grandmother, singing this hymn.

He recovers during the next song, which is unfamiliar, and sits gratefully at the end of all the singing. "It should be over pretty soon now," he reasons to himself. Next, they baptize a baby, which is sweet. Especially when on the big video screen he can see the water dribbling over the baby's fuzzy head, and the tiny gasp of surprise it produces. The people all say "yes" out loud when the pastor asks if they'll take care of this baby as it grows up in the church. This strikes him as sincere and noble. He tries to think of the last time he witnessed something sincere or noble, and can't come up with anything.

Another pastor is kneeling to pray, and the lights go dim. He sucks in a deep breath and is glad for a break in the action. He hears the pastor saying, "…in the words he taught us to pray…" and that familiar prayer starts. He can't remember it but, since he's never closed his eyes, he notices the words going up on screen. He joins at "…hallowed be thy name…"

———◎◎◎———

Defining the Principle of Meaning

The principle of meaning is exactly what it seems to be. It is the idea that our work has merit on its own and can add value to worship beyond technical support. In many church settings, the media ministry functions only as a technical support ministry to provide sound amplification, projected lyrics and liturgy, and video or graphics for sermons. The technical team simply executes, making sure the technical pieces are in place and run as prescribed. In many churches, there is little or no effort to use the tools in a meaningful way.

This approach has merit and is the best one for some churches, at certain stages. In a new or very small church, the pastor may design his or her own graphics for the sermon and may simply need a volunteer to run the presentation. There may not be staff or volunteers to do more planning and production than this. And there may not yet be the need for it. When a church is starting out, especially, it's important to do only what can be done well, and that may be as simple as a few pages of projected graphics during the sermon. The tech team model is valid in some very large churches, as well. Here, the media ministry may be structured to include a technical team that's responsible solely for execution. As the ministry grows, it can be organized into function-based teams, with teams responsible for creative content and media production, and separate teams responsible for event production and execution. Execution, implementation, support of other ministries, and customer service—to phrase it in a secular-world way—are critical functions of the media ministry. But in addition, in most churches, media can and should be used with meaning.

So, what *kind* of meaning? And where do we get it? Think for a minute about the first four principles. There you'll find the substance and the source for meaning in media. Meaning is tied to purpose and is framed by the values, culture, and vision of your church. It is the very idea that you can and should use your media ministry to communicate these things to your congregation.

In this chapter, we'll examine the principle of meaning. We'll discuss some ways media can add real value to your church's worship services, with examples on the DVD accompanying this book. And you'll learn how to apply the principle in the way you run your media ministry, avoiding the obstacles that can get in the way of your ability to produce media with meaning.

> Meaning is tied to purpose and is framed by the values, culture, and vision of your church. It is the very idea that you can and should use your media ministry to communicate these things to your congregation.

Meaning and Purpose

Media should add value to your church's worship, based on your church's purpose, values, culture, and vision. It should take what's already happening there and up the ante, increase the impact, and propel the message so that it goes further and deeper into the hearts and minds of the congregation. Video should enhance, enlarge, illustrate, and amplify. Meaningful media should move the congregation from one place in worship to another—from shallow understanding to depth, from complacency to conviction, from passivity to engagement. Conversely, media should never subtract from the overall substance and impact of worship; the congregation should not be confused, offended, or worn out by the use of video or other media.

Media ministries typically function simply as service-providers. We'll address this later in the chapter, but I believe that this particular model is shortsighted, in most instances. It can even be self-defeating not to do media with meaning. It gives the congregation, which in many churches is already skeptical, reason to dislike media in their worship services. If your use of media does not add value to the service and simply serves as eye-catching wallpaper, then what's it there for? On the other hand, if media adds a layer of meaning, moves the congregation to understand more deeply, and elicits a new feeling, then people will be more likely to embrace it. In the story

> Meaningful media should move the congregation from one place in worship to another—from shallow understanding to depth, from complacency to conviction, from passivity to engagement.

that opened this chapter, the man was representative of that church's target audience—unchurched, skeptical, and resistant. The thoughtful, intentional use of media in that worship service added meaning to the experience, which in the end he could not ignore. Media compelled him to participate and engage in worship. In a church where the purpose is to reach unchurched people, media with meaning helps to fulfill that purpose.

About "Wallpaper"

In some mainline churches, especially, wallpaper is important! What does your sanctuary look like? If it predates *The Godfather* Watergate, and the first reign of the lava lamp, it might be a beautiful building. Stone-masonry walls, arched wooden beams, frescoed motifs, needlepoint kneeling-rail cushions, hand-carved pews, and stained glass windows. Some of us ache, at times, for a glimmer of light through a stained glass window. Christendom's beautiful old churches are a treasure, but present obvious challenges for media ministries. On the other hand, post-lava-lamp buildings are generally more accommodating to projectors and screens, but they lack aesthetic appeal. This is where beautiful wallpaper comes in, in the form of projected or printed-paper or textile images. In some of our rather plain, boxy, windowless buildings, the media ministry can provide color, warmth, rich visual interest, and texture, in addition to meaning. Wallpaper probably shouldn't be your ministry's reason for being, but it can be a valuable function.

Meaning and Style

In my own ministry, the idea of producing meaningful media for worship has always been central, and style is part of the quotient. I began my career as a video producer, interested in stories and ideas and feelings and human motivation. I love working with images, words, and music. We've developed a style for main weekend worship. Someone once dubbed it "swoopy", which does seem to fit. Most of the video produced has a somewhat classical look. It's not trendy, and it is deceptively simple looking. We use many layers in the edit process, and we use effects that are not immediately recognizable as effects, creating a subtly polished feel. Our graphics are standardized, steering away from kitschy fonts or effected text.

An example, found on the DVD accompanying this book, is the *Change a Life* clip from a video produced for a stewardship campaign. We added a whitewash layer and a couple of other effects to this video, which is comprised of testimonials. For titles, we used a classic font (Palatino) over a white background. For video transitions, we dipped to white rather than black. The overall feel we hoped to elicit was an ethereal, dreamy, poignant one. This was our goal for a couple of reasons. The campaign was to raise funds for the first year in a new sanctuary, so we were asking our congregation to take a faithful step forward in their giving. It was a "dreamy" time for the church, as the congregation faced amazing new opportunities together. And it was poignant, because we had just lost a well-known member to cancer. This young man and his wife had just had their first child. He was deeply involved in the church and was a classic Church of the Resurrection story—he met and committed his life to Christ in this congregation. The style of that video captured the collective heart of the congregation at that moment in time and added a rich layer of meaning to that year's stewardship campaign.

Meaning and Intentionality

Media with meaning requires intentionality. A get-it-done-quick approach will rarely result in value-added projects for worship. A simple thing like choosing a background for lyrics can make a difference; it takes time and thought and requires risk, but it is worth the effort. Media is a powerful tool, and if we're blessed to have it, we should use it well. Otherwise, it's sort of like having a top-of-the-line, loaded computer and only using the calculator function. One tricky thing to remember about meaning is that often people will not consciously notice the difference. Those added layers of detail and thoughtfulness will alter and enrich the congregation's experience. They may not walk away saying, "Wow, that service had a lovely luminous feel from the animated stained glass video background behind that classical-looking font during the worship songs!" But your work will have a subconscious impact.

Meaning is rooted in purpose and is wrapped in values, culture, and vision. Style helps us create meaningful projects. And we must be intentional about producing media with meaning. Let's look now at some examples of meaning as applied in the work itself.

Applying Meaning in Your Ministry's Work

As Christians, we hope everything we do is meaningful. That's what we strive for, at least. In our work with media ministry, we should hope for the same. "Meaningful worship" is a key value of worship planning at many churches. Teams meet weekly in churches across the country, sweating over timing and liturgy and themes and symbols, to bring meaning to that hour of worship each weekend, to make every moment count. For most of us in the established denominations, this effort is well placed. In this section, we'll look at examples of the principle of meaning as applied in actual projects, including examples from Church of the Resurrection and from other church settings. You'll find the Resurrection examples on the DVD accompanying this book.

The Iconographic Image

The idea of the Iconographic Image developed naturally and unintentionally. As I produced one or two video projects per year for the church as a volunteer, I found that there were a tiny handful of images—footage I'd shot of church activities—that came to have greater meaning and stronger power than we'd normally expect. These images seemed to draw in all the people watching them, binding the congregation together in some sort of mysterious way. (I believe it's the Holy Spirit, working through a camera lens, an edit system, and a projector.) These shots are often not the most well-framed or color-balanced or well-lit on the reel. In fact, the images from the early years were shot on VHS and looked pretty horrid even in the 1990s. However, when we play these scenes, you can feel the congregation's reaction. It's palpable. Iconographic Images do something extraordinary: *They create shared memory.* This has an amazing effect on two groups of people in your congregation, the newbies and the old-timers.

For people who are new to your congregation, the Iconographic Image is almost like a time machine, taking them back to pivotal events in the church's past with people who experienced those events. It's a way of saying, "Come on, let's go back. You can experience what we experienced, and it will be as if you were there with us." Iconographic Images allow new members of your church family to share memories that they don't really share.

> Iconographic Images allow new members of your church family to share memories that they don't really share.

For longtime members, these images have a different but equally important effect. We know that, as a church grows, some of the people most at risk of falling away are the ones who were there at the beginning. Iconographic Images remind these members why they've devoted so much to the congregation over the years. These images honor them and honor the past, which, especially for people struggling with change in the church, sometimes seems brighter than the future. Iconographic Images are a sort of intimate invitation to feel attached to the church and to claim a sense of belonging for the first time, or once again. They remind us of who we are and where we've come from as a church family.

These images have been critical at our church; you'll find several examples of them on the DVD. As you move forward in your ministry, I encourage you to shoot video and/or take still photos at church events. You probably will not see these moments coming, because sometimes we don't recognize that we're in the middle of a pivotal moment until it's past. And the importance of an image will often dawn on you some time after you've shot the footage. But be on the lookout for images of people and events that seem to visually crystallize something important about your church—a program, a value, a vision, or your purpose. These will become your church's Iconographic Images. Resist the temptation to overuse them. Use them once or twice each year, when you're asking the congregation to consider big picture ideas—a change in the church's vision, a re-commitment to the purpose, the introduction of a new value. These are times when your congregation needs to bind together, and well-used Iconographic Images will help do that.

> Be on the lookout for images of people and events that seem to visually crystallize something important about your church—a program, a value, a vision, or your purpose.

Examples of Meaning Applied in Work

Advent

- One year for Advent our theme was "There Is A Light At The End…" We chose to use candles and candlelight as our main thematic visual element. We talked about many other themes and visual representations during our planning meetings in the early fall. When we settled in on the "light" idea, we decided to narrow it down to candlelight. Candlelight is a powerful symbol of Christmas, so it seemed to be a natural fit. As we considered the style of our media for this series, we wanted something warm, inviting, and welcoming. We wanted to create a feeling that we were enfolding the congregation in Emmanuel. Candlelight would do the trick. But how do you bring candlelight into the service without giving the congregation candles, which we save for Candlelight Christmas Eve? We pulled out an old set of banners with the Advent themes—Hope, Peace, Joy, Love—emblazoned in rich jewel tones, with lots of purple. Each banner was framed by an abstract candle design, sewn in metallic gold fabric. These banners were our starting point; they hung along the walls of the chancel area.

- There are stock photos of candles all over the place on the web, available for downloading. However, as we talked about the projects and thought about the qualities of candlelight, the movement of the flame was itself something that seemed important. That movement gives the candle life and interest. Look at a still photo of a candle, and then look at moving video of a candle. There's a big difference in the feeling elicited between the two versions. We chose to shoot video. The producer and videographer spent a lot of time on this: meeting to plan logistics, shopping for dozens and dozens of candles, setting up the shot in the studio, shooting (three days), and editing the footage (more than three days) to make it work as backgrounds for graphics. They also set up and shot video of a purple velvet drape, which we used to create a bar for our lower-third graphics. The purple is, of course, symbolic of Christ's reign as King; it pulled color into the graphics design and linked the graphics with the banners. Was it worth it? Yes. The moving video behind lyrics, Scripture, and liturgy, and at other times rolling on its own without text, achieved what we hoped it would. It created a warm environment in the middle of snowstorms and provided a continual reminder of the central symbol for our Advent worship, the Light of Christ.

'Wesley' Sermon Series

- In the early planning for a three-part series on John Wesley, we reviewed portraits of Wesley, which are somewhat uninspiring. Excerpts from his sermons and other writings were to be a central part of the sermons, and the aim was to draw the congregation into a real sense of who Wesley was, what we can learn from him today, and his importance to Methodism. We had a quandary. How can we bring someone to life when there are no video clips, no photos, and only a few uninspiring pictures of him? We considered the power of his words and decided to concentrate on those. We decided to create the *feeling* of Wesley and to acknowledge the congregation's probable sense of curiosity about him. We recruited a volunteer from our ministry who was about Wesley's size and stature. We hired a voice-over actor who was originally from England. We secured use of a small, old chapel surrounded by English gardens about an hour away from Kansas City. Then, we set about creating a series of dreamlike scenes showing "John Wesley" reading, writing, praying, preaching, walking, and thinking in and around the chapel and countryside. We shot these in an intentionally non-realistic way—out of focus, from behind, zeroing in on details like hands or feet. This was to avoid any sense of realism and cue the congregation that this was a vision of what Wesley's days might have been like. Our pastor selected the excerpts for each week's sermon, which our English actor read as voice-over—he even used the correct Wesley dialect, to be authentic. So each weekend, the congregation saw a dreamlike depiction of John Wesley and heard "Wesley's voice" reading his own sermons, journal entries, and letters. This required a lot of planning and time in production but added real value to the congregation's ability to engage their own curiosity, to learn about Wesley, and to act (we hope) on what they learned.

- Another example of meaning found on the DVD is from a capital campaign to raise funds for a new sanctuary, narthex, and children's education wing. The piece entitled "How Far Can You See" uses five members of the congregation as spokespersons to explain the vision for the new facility. Using these folks creates a non-intimidating feel, highlights a sense of community, and is effectively appealing. The last shot in the piece is of five chairs arranged as if in a church row, except that the chairs are sitting in the large field where the building will be erected. The new sanctuary will hold three thousand of the seats. The overriding image and theme of the campaign was to create room—literally seats in the sanctuary—for the new people who might visit and join our church. In this final shot, the camera is on a crane. The shot starts out on the five spokespeople clustered together, delivering their last lines. As the people walk toward the camera, it pulls up and out. The people walk out of frame as the camera reveals the five chairs. The last line asks the congregation, "How far can we see?" reinforcing the idea that God has plans for us and that it is now our task to grasp that vision and to faithfully take steps to bring it to fruition. The chairs are a literal illustration of that vision of God's plan for the church. Symbolism is powerful. Use it to add meaning to your media in worship.

- Note: The next two examples are used earlier in the book, but they provide good illustration of ways to apply the principle of meaning, too. So I'll describe them again here.
- During one fall we did a series of sermons on the denominations of Christianity. Again, we spent many hours generating ideas around this topic. We finally settled on the visual theme of stained glass windows. This theme provided a great way for us to add meaning to the media in those services. Stained glass was important in part because it harkens back to the feel of traditional worship, which we were celebrating in that series. It signifies one of the things we tried to do with the series, which was to honor some of the major denominations—Orthodox, Roman Catholic, Anglican, Presbyterian, Lutheran, Pentecostal, Baptist, and Methodist. Our aim was to lift from each something that could enrich our own worship. We wanted the series to have a noble, beautiful, tradition-filled sensibility. One problem for us was that we have no stained glass in our building! We hired an illustrator and provided him with a set of important symbols for each denomination. He created a series of separate panels drawn in pen, ink, and watercolors to closely resemble stained glass. Each panel represented one denomination, and the panels fit together to create one unified arched window. This in itself added a layer of symbolic meaning. We used the illustration to create a series of banners for the chancel walls; when lit, they really looked like stained glass windows. And we animated the illustration with layered video effects to create a moving background hinting at the movement of light across richly colored windows in a church. All of

this required extra thought and time but gave a beautiful, noble, luminous quality to each week's services. The visuals clearly underscored the theme and teachings and helped the congregation to remember what they had learned.

- In the fall of that same year, we turned to Proverbs for another eight-week sermon series. This time, we hoped to create a different layer of meaning. In his sermon notes, the pastor wondered if interviewing a few of the older folks in the congregation to get their perspective on wisdom, the central theme in Proverbs, would work. We took that idea and developed it into the visuals for the series. We concentrated on the visual themes of age and nature—the human beauty that comes with age, and the cyclical beauty we find in nature. We shot the interviews with some of our congregation's elder sages at a local arboretum, where they were surrounded by trees. The sermon series was titled, "Pathway to Wisdom"; we framed the interview subjects with leaf-strewn paths heading into the woods behind them, and we shot footage of the subjects meandering along the paths. We purchased photos of autumn leaves in several different configurations to coordinate with our arboretum interview setting, and used these for the bulletin cover, chancel banners, and graphics backgrounds. Everything about the series was earthy, warm, and natural, as if the whole thing had literally taken root in our church.

A few other general ideas…

- If you use graphics in worship, what do you project at the end of your service? Instead of the uninspired throw-away "Have a Nice Day" or "Thanks for Worshiping With Us" slide, try this: Choose an excerpt from the day's sermon or Scripture, or a line from the closing hymn. Choose only one sentence or phrase. Try to make this the one thing you'd like the congregation to take away, if they could only remember one thing. Add this to your graphics package to add a little nugget of meaning.

- If you run a monthly or weekly news-style video during your worship services (or before or at Sunday School or another time and place), consider your "talent." Who serves as the spokesperson for these announcements? Try using regular congregation members. This deflates the feeling of overproduced glitz that these pieces sometimes have. The real person gives it a feeling of community, personal involvement, and buy-in. And nearly every church has at least a person or two who can memorize a few lines of on-camera copy, and then can read the rest as voice-over. Your announcements will take on a vibrant authenticity—meaning—with this technique.

• When you project biblical text, how intentional are you about the way you format the words? So much of the Bible is poetry, and it's meant to be seen that way. When you project a psalm, be careful to mimic the indentation, spacing, and punctuation you find in your Bible. The congregation will learn more about the Scriptures, and their experience of them in worship will be richer.

Many churches use the technique of metaphor with great success. The media ministry team at Ginghamsburg United Methodist Church pioneered the application of metaphor in media.[4] Two members of that team, Len Wilson and Jason Moore, now produce great work that is available for other churches. It's possible to develop metaphors to the point where nearly every element in worship is linked somehow. Metaphor, like symbolism, can effectively add meaning to worship media. It creates a hook, which is helpful in worship planning and in production. And metaphor leaves something for congregants to take with them as they leave the church—sometimes literally.

Humor can also add meaning in worship, but this is tricky. The preaching pastor should be very comfortable with humor before you use it. And in our mainline churches, where tradition is typically valued and reverence is the rule, humor almost always needs to be doled out in small amounts. Humor is an awesome community-builder and icebreaker. People-on-the-street-style interviews, where random folks are videotaped answering questions are common in worship and can be fun and lighthearted, while still making a point. Used judiciously, humor can add a delightful layer of meaning.

In some churches, an edgy, almost counter-cultural, random style is important in adding meaning. The church's purpose, values, culture, and vision will dictate style to a great degree. Because that sort of style is a departure from tradition, especially for many mainline churches, it becomes imbued with its own inherent meaning. The style itself repre-

---

[4] See *Out on the Edge*, or *The Wired Church*, or *Handbook for Multisensory Worship*, vols 1 and 2 (Nashville: Abingdon Press, 1997-2001).

sents what the congregation is about, who they're hoping to reach, or what they see as God's mission for them in the world.

A similar example is found in what's been dubbed the Emergent church. Here, media is more about creating a feeling in worship, an environment. That visual environment is more important in this setting than our traditional, linear, text-based presentation. Meaning in this context is boiled down, essential. And in many cases what's essential is left open-ended, not all neatly tied up, with questions left lingering.

In churches experimenting with other forms and styles of worship, media isn't based so much on technical mechanisms as on tactile ones. New Orthodox congregations and others find meaning in print, art, fabric, textiles, and paper hung from ceilings and walls, used as banners and bulletins, or actually placed in the hands of the congregation. Meaning here is derived from the physical experience of feeling something, or from the sensation of sharing space with something. Icons and other visual symbols can be important in this setting, too. Here, meaning is based on experience, pared down but still drawn from ancient worship traditions.[5]

Applying Meaning in the Formation and Operation of Your Ministry

In this section, we'll explore some final points about meaning in worship media. First, we'll look at what's required to produce media with meaning, with an example illustrating all the requirements at once. Then, we'll discuss some obstacles that can get in the way of meaning.

What Is Required?

Producing media for worship with meaning requires:

- An understanding of the purpose, values, culture, and vision of your church; these principles should shape and direct the meaning in your work
- Intentionality and thoughtfulness
- Time to plan ahead
- Commitment to a creative process, willingness to risk

---

[5] See Catherine Kapikian, *Art In Service of the Sacred* (Nashville: Abingdon Press, 2006).

Here's an example of how each of these requirements came into play during one Advent season: The sermon production team created an idea for sermon openers, using the candlelight video (discussed earlier in this chapter). The Advent sermon series title was "The Light at the End..." signifying the light (Christ) at the end of the tunnel (our human condition). The idea involved setting up the human condition each week just before the sermon, using a child's voice saying a prayer. The prayers encapsulated, from a child's perspective, the week's "tunnel"—hopelessness about the future and our world, discontent, and the joylessness we sometimes experience in life. The team wrote scripts, recorded the voice-over prayers, and loaded the candle footage into the editor. They put together a rough cut for review two weeks before the start of Advent. It started in black, with a small glimmer of candlelight in one corner. The candlelight multiplied and grew as we heard the child's voice asking God about that week's troublesome issue. At the "amen," the candlelight slowly swelled to fill the frame with softly, slowly flickering flames. The scriptural answer to that prayer dissolved on screen in silence, ending the piece in hope.

The piece went together exactly as planned, and was well executed in every way. But when we sat in the edit room and looked at the finished piece, we realized that it would not work in the worship services. It would certainly add meaning, but it would add the wrong kind. When played back, the video felt too somber and focused on the negative. The pastor felt this too and struggled to figure out how to get comfortable with it. That was a good signal to bail. If the preaching pastor has to work around a piece, or must work to make it fit, the piece should probably not be used, at least not as part of the sermon. In this case, we still had our Plan B. We simply used the moving candle video as backgrounds for Scripture, along with shots of art, maps, and other graphics used in the sermons. The sermons were following the lectionary, and Scripture was important in the series; so focusing on the text and highlighting it with beautiful backgrounds made sense.

> The creative process requires failures. And these really are not failures so much as they are results of the risk inherent in trying something new.

The creative process requires failures of this kind. And these really are not failures so much as they are results of the risk inherent in trying something new. As we watched the child's prayer clip, we realized that it would have an unintended impact on our congregation and possibly on the preacher. The congregation, many of whom were new to church and slightly uncomfortable to begin with, would feel like they were being manipulated before the sermon even began. By showing the video, we would raise their hackles and risk losing their engagement at that moment. And we'd have a pastor who was preaching something not from his heart.

In this example, the team needed to understand the purpose and culture of our congregation. They thought intentionally about how the piece might work, and they had a backup plan in case the experiment failed. They gave themselves plenty of time to try the idea before committing to it, which required planning ahead for all the logistics. And they were committed to their creative process, willing to risk. They were willing to spend the time, resources, and energy necessary, and they were willing to extend themselves creatively, with no guarantee of success.

Obstacles to Meaning

(1) Intolerance to Risk

Many things can get in the way of our ability to produce media with meaning. One barrier is intolerance to risk. The process required to produce something meaningful—to add that extra layer that helps push a message into the congregant's heart—requires you to step out in faith creatively. There is nothing new under the sun, and at times it sure seems like there are no new ideas floating around. But I think the context around us makes old ideas new and gives them new application. You might have seen a graphic technique work in one setting, but you may not be sure if it will work in your own setting. Furthermore, if an idea is new to you, it is new. If you envision a new way to use video during praise and worship in your church, it is new. Some of us instinctively shove those new ideas aside, relying on what's tried, true, and safe. For some, the chance that we might spend time, thought, and resources on something for naught is a deal-killer. For others, that risk is part of the fun; this is so for me. It's almost a sense that the journey is the destination, although not quite; for all of us, worship is the destination. There's a challenge for all of us in this issue of risk. If you're a person who needs to know what you can count on and feels most comfortable when things go exactly as planned, you might need to find or bring someone on your team who can gently press you to risk a bit more. Otherwise, your work might become staid and even stale, with thinner and thinner layers of meaning. For those of us who are more risk-tolerant, we must be careful not to trample

The context around us makes old ideas new and gives them new application.

others in the process. Even other risk-takers can become irritated if all the risks are at someone else's direction and their own ideas are never tried. And in every group there are likely to be people who work better within structure and regularity. Creative risk-takers need to find ways to tone down the adventure. We all must compromise. The most creative and productive teams seem to be those with a combination of risk-takers and risk-resistors. When things are humming along in this setting, everyone has great ideas, spurred on by the takers. And the production cycle runs smoothly, kept in check by the resistors.

(2) Poor Planning

Media, music, liturgy, preaching, prayer, sacraments, and other elements work together in worship. Each element has its place and appeals to different people at different times. Sometimes, some elements work better than others. But they work best when they're planned to go together, forming a cohesive, impactful, God-honoring whole. Most churches have a worship-planning team of some sort. It's important to have a model for worship planning that allows for creativity and intentionality.

Plan to Create

Creativity and intentionality are important. Your worship services and the media you produce for them will be easier to implement, and more engaging for the congregation, if you spend time regularly in thoughtful planning. Use sermon series; metaphor; season-based themes, or themes based on church programs, activities, or events; or use the lectionary. Use some sort of theme to connect worship from service to service for at least three or four weeks. This enables you to spend more time and energy on a theme, because that theme will last a few weeks; this is more efficient and effective than planning everything new each week. Also use the theme to link elements to one another within worship. Your services will take on a cohesiveness that helps drive the message home to the congregation, and you'll have a chance at planning more creative worship if you're planning one theme per month, rather than one per week.

Poor planning leads to disjointed and less effective worship. The individual elements—a song, liturgy, prayer, sermon, or video—might be effective, but the whole is less so without the right type and amount of planning. Another result of poor planning is that media becomes relegated to basic support only. You've got to have time to plan and produce good media; you can't do that if you are not planning ahead. If you already have some tools and the capacity to produce good work—even if monthly instead of weekly—you should carve out the planning time required. Otherwise, you're wasting what you have.

A third result of poor planning takes us back to chapter 5: Excellence. Good media can't be improvised like music sometimes can. Planning and implementing media takes not only time but also skill. At its worst, media in worship is of poor quality and adds no value to worship; distracting and confusing, it devalues the experience. Poor planning decreases your chance of creating meaningful media.

(3) Lack of Collaborative Effort

The planning process involves people and time. I've seen many different configurations for worship planning and have worked within several models myself. What I'll describe in this section is what I believe makes the most sense for the greatest number of churches. But the ideas here are meant to help you think about your own planning and collaboration, or lack thereof. My hope is that something here will make perfect sense or at least generate a new idea for your ministry. The terms and titles used here may not apply exactly to your setting, so infer as necessary to interpret for your church. My basic conclusion is that collaborative planning requires a handful of different teams that intersect at critical points then spin off on their own for a time. Those teams are: (1) the small creative, or content, design team, (2) the larger worship-planning team, and (3) the individual teams for execution, which include media, music, clergy, preaching pastor, and other staff. As media ministries grow, it is often helpful to have separate teams responsible for design and execution. The skills required for each are divergent; people who are good at generating ideas are often not the best at figuring out how to actually make them happen. These teams need to intersect, too, with at least one person sitting on both to make sure the right hand knows what the left hand just decided to do next weekend! (An important assumption underlying this process is that your preaching pastor is planning sermons several weeks—preferably many months—ahead of time and that this information is provided to all those involved in worship planning.)

Worship-planning Team

First, we'll examine the worship-planning team. This team includes those in your church who have particular expertise or wisdom, an important perspective, or some influence on what happens in worship. This group probably should not exceed fifteen to eighteen people in the largest church settings, and it should be much smaller, perhaps eight to ten people, in medium-sized churches. (Remember, these are just guidelines; bend them to fit.) The idea here is to gather people who will add value to the preliminary discussions about a worship series. Included should be the preacher, music and media directors, and anyone else who is a part of the design team sketched out below. Additionally, the team might include other pastors, musicians, media team members, artists, and worship committee members as well as thoughtful and interesting people from the congregation. This group should meet one or two weeks prior to the design team meeting (described below). *The purpose of their meeting is to generate perspectives, context, and varied frames of reference for the worship series being discussed.*

The group may change depending on the subject matter. For instance, if you're planning a series of worship services aimed at edifying young families, you might include the Children's Ministry Director and a couple of young parents on the team for that series. This meeting should provide a lot of ideas for those on the design team. Book titles, CDs, movies, photos, artwork, prayers, essays—these can all be brought forward for consideration. This is big-picture input time. Then, the winnowing begins...

Content-design Team

Next, let's look at the creative, or content, design team. *This team is made up of those who are primarily responsible for what goes on in worship* and should include the fewest people possible, preferably no more than five or six. These are the people who have, as part of their job descriptions (whether paid or unpaid staff), the greatest degree of influence on worship. The person who drives most of the decision-making and vision-casting for worship, typically the preaching pastor, should be on this team. Additionally, the team should include persons responsible for decision-making on music, media, and any other elements that are a regular part of worship—another pastor or liturgist, musicians (both contemporary and traditional), people involved with drama and dance, and others. This team should meet many weeks before the start of each new phase of worship, whether that means a new sermon series, liturgical season, or something else. For most churches, the number of weeks out will be between six and twelve, depending on the complexity of your services. *The purpose of this meeting is to generate ideas for every element in worship during that series or phase.* The group will have had time to sort through all the fodder from the earlier worship planning team meeting. The team should generate ideas, free of judgment.

They should come back together one or two weeks later, each having thought about the ideas. At this time, they should narrow down the focus to one idea, theme, or direction for the series. If possible in the time allotted, the team should nail down some specifics—sketches, pictures or photos for reference, actual song titles, prayers, or other liturgy.

Implementation Teams

After all of the people on the design team have their individual marching orders, they go back to their respective teams and set to work. Musicians order music and begin rehearsing. Clergy begin searching for or writing liturgy and prayers. The media team begins scriptwriting, shooting, designing graphics, editing, and so on. The design team should meet every couple of weeks or more to check whether everything is still on track and to make changes as needed. And the implementation teams from each ministry area should meet weekly to coordinate all the logistics required to execute the design team's plan. This should include those responsible for audio, graphics, video playback, and lighting; any other technical team members; and those responsible for execution in music and other areas. By two weeks before each service, most of the details should be completed, ready to go. Each week the implementation team is double-checking to make sure that everything is set to the greatest degree possible. Your definition of excellence will play a big role in determining exactly what that means and how far in advance you should be able to get set.

This is a very rough sketch of one model for worship planning. Assuming that you're using some sort of functional worship-planning model, let's talk about creative collaboration and the creative process. These are what should happen in the meetings described above.

The purpose of the large worship planning group is to generate initial input for the design team, however, this group is not responsible for the final idea. This large team serves as an advisory panel for discussion. The idea is to get a broad base and a wide variety of perspectives. But these perspectives must get funneled down to that which is most important. And whatever rises to the top as being most important must be shaped and refined into something compelling and effective—whatever that means in your setting. That's where the funnel must go from wide to narrow, from the large input-giving group to the small design-generating group. *Note: One person should lead or facilitate these groups, and it should be the person who'll do the best job of driving ideas along, keeping the floor open, and maintaining an open discussion environment. That may or may not be the "highest-ranked" person at the table.* The narrowing-down process requires so many meetings because it takes several passes for each person to hear ideas, think about them, zero in on one or two, generate new ideas, and so on and so forth. This process ends when the team either lands on *the* idea, or runs out of time and has to pull the trigger on something.

Creative by Committee (No!)

It's tempting (and I know this from personal experience) to whittle away at the meetings, shoehorn people and purposes into one two-hour-long weekly worship-planning meeting, and just hope you get to most of the critical stuff. Though I've proposed a lot of meetings, I also know that "creative by committee" doesn't work. That's why I recommend keeping the design team to no more than six people, if at all possible. Often when a larger group of people becomes involved in doing the design work, the ideas become diluted or suppressed. Some people clam up, fearing they'll make fools of themselves. Others simply feel uncomfortable sharing ideas in large groups or with people they don't know well. Still others believe that their ideas, or the ways they might articulate them, are simply inferior to all the others at the table, so why waste everyone's time? In a small, close-knit group, people feel safe to offer ideas and are less likely to censor their thoughts, feelings, and words. Trust is absolutely vital in this equation. It takes time to develop, but that sense of absolute trust, of authentic brotherly or sisterly love, is critical if we are to do our best worship planning. The design team should strive for small-group honesty and authentic discussion. The persons on the team should be open and willing to share with one another. They should function in a secure atmosphere of unity, support, and friendly teamwork. Each person should be able to risk in this environment, secure in the knowledge that the small group around the table will listen with openness, respect, grace, and anticipation of great things. In a healthy small group, you end up with many interesting ideas on the table at the end of the session.

Also, style is important. And it's difficult for a large group of people to agree on or even understand the same style. The important sensibility of style, look, and feel in worship should be focused and consistent, in order to contribute to meaningful media. In my experience, that only comes from a handful of people who, over time, begin to see things in similar ways. Remember the child's game "Telephone"? One person starts with a simple message then passes it on to the next, who passes it on to the next. By the end of the game, the original message becomes distorted and is sometimes completely unrecognizable. Similarly, it's tough for more than a few people to really share a specific idea. Remember this other child's game—making mud pies? "Creative by committee" just muddies things up.

On the other hand, we do need creative collaboration. Iron sharpens iron, and good ideas rarely spring from a vacuum. Good ideas beget good ideas. An excellent pastor, like the one I've been privileged to serve under, will generate ideas in his or her sermon planning notes. The production team takes these, tosses them around, tweaks them, and adds to them. The pastor then takes the revised batch and further refines it. In my experience, we nearly always make one another's ideas better. That's why I advocate this team-based approach.

(4) Tail Wagging

Another obstacle to creating meaningful media for worship is our natural tendency to do fun stuff just because we can. Is the tail wagging the dog? It's easy to slip into this, especially as your ministry grows and your church acquires new toys. This typically happens when we concentrate on the technology rather than on things like the principles in this book. That's when we daydream about the dazzling effects we can now create with the latest software update, or whatever. When we get wrapped up in *what* our tools can do, rather than *why* we're doing it, we get into this trouble.

> When we get wrapped up in what our tools can do, rather than why we're doing it, we get into this trouble.

- Tail-wagging-the-dog wastes resources of every kind. It's simply bad stewardship. Form should follow function, and media should serve its purpose, not the other way around.

- Doing what's cool and new, just because you can, backfires. Too often, churches get new equipment and go wild with their blossoming technical capabilities, hardly attending to things like purpose or vision or culture. But technology-driven ideas don't often work. It's as if the media was applied to the worship service like a gaudy, sequined sticker, instead of planned as an integral part of the worship service. The congregation sees this and is confused, distracted, or put off by it. These tech teams get swatted back rather often, when the members rightly complain that the technical stuff has not only failed to add value to worship but has actually become an obstacle itself.

- Tail-wagging creates frustration for staff and volunteers. The pastor may feel compelled to use an element in order to save someone from hurt feelings and to honor his or her time. But this doesn't really serve anyone, certainly not the congregation. The pastor either preaches around something that doesn't work well or feels guilty for canning an element. The staff and volunteers may see their time and effort as having been wasted, and they may end up feeling demoralized. And it's frustrating for all concerned to see unused video, graphics, and other media sitting in the can, so to speak, on the shelf, collecting dust.

Media ministry leaders should define and set parameters for what is truly meaningful, based on the purpose, values, culture, and vision of the church, and they must communicate this to others.

A Final Thought

Media is what we do, and it has limitations. We may yearn sometimes for a beautiful, stone, gothic-style church like the one where I grew up. Or we may long for a simple, sweet, white clapboard church with wide wooden shutters and a tin-roofed bell tower, like the one I sometimes attend during the summer near Lake Michigan. We may want to go to a place that has no sound amplification or video screens but only the closeness of human voices, reading and singing from hymnals, prayer books, and Bibles. But here we are, striving to serve Christ in this time and in this place. And there are moments when, either solely or in part because of media, we feel the nudging presence of the Holy Spirit, or we understand something in a new way, or we feel convicted to take some action. In those moments we know that God intends to use this tool to deepen people's faith, to reach those who don't yet know him and draw them to him. God will reach many people with this tool. We are privileged! And we are responsible for using the tool well.

> "It's like a man going off on an extended trip. He called his servants together and delegated responsibilities. To one he gave five thousand dollars, to another two thousand, to a third one thousand, depending on their abilities. Then he left. Right off, the first servant went to work and doubled his master's investment. The second did the same. But the man with the single thousand dug a hole and carefully buried his master's money.

"After a long absence, the master of those three servants came back and settled up with them. The one given five thousand dollars showed him how he had doubled his investment. His master commended him: 'Good work! You did your job well. From now on be my partner.'

"The servant with the two thousand showed how he also had doubled his master's investment. His master commended him: 'Good work! You did your job well. From now on be my partner.'

"The servant given one thousand said, 'Master, I know you have high standards and hate careless ways, that you demand the best and make no allowances for error. I was afraid I might disappoint you, so I found a good hiding place and secured your money. Here it is, safe and sound down to the last cent.'

"The master was furious. 'That's a terrible way to live! It's criminal to live cautiously like that! If you knew I was after the best, why did you do less than the least? The least you could have done would have been to invest the sum with the bankers, where at least I would have gotten a little interest.

'Take the thousand and give it to the one who risked the most. And get rid of this "play-it-safe" who won't go out on a limb. Throw him out into utter darkness.'

Matthew 25:14–30 (The Message)

Our Master has high standards, and we are fearful of disappointing. Sometimes it seems smarter to be cautious, to play it safe. And our work is ceaseless, ever changing, always challenging, and often perplexing. But I pray for you that it is also rewarding and that you feel God's pleasure in your efforts. It is difficult to keep ego out of our work and to keep Christ at its center. I pray that you will find ways to do so. It is the most important principle for any ministry and is the root of the principles laid out in this book. Finally, I pray for you the boldness to go out on a limb, to invest your time and your passion in this ministry. You already have the most awesome partner.

Questions for Media Ministry Planning

(1) Are we doing this just because we can?

(2) Will this element (video, graphics, print, or whatever) subtract from the overall substance and impact of worship?

(3) Could the congregation be at all confused or offended by this?

(4) Is it too much, too heavy-handed, or too over-the-top stylistically? Is the congregation likely to be worn out at the end of it? (This might be the desired outcome; just make sure to do a gut check if it's not.)

(5) What value will this add to worship, exactly?

(6) Does this illustrate a point, enlarge our understanding, or enhance our experience in some meaningful way?

(7) Does this element move the congregation in some way, taking people from shallow understanding to depth, complacency to conviction, or passivity to engagement?

(8) Where can we improve the intentionality of our planning process?

(9) Is our current planning process working?

Postscript

The tall, lanky man is real. He was raised in a church and attended weekly. He walked away from God in college, freed of the constraints and what he perceived as the hypocrisy and inconsistencies of a church that seemed meaningless and irrelevant in his life and in the world. Not long after we met, he told me that the video screens captured him during his first visit to the church. They were unexpected. The graphics and video were well executed, which was important for this highly educated skeptic. The use of media added value to the experience for him. Media in worship wasn't the only reason he agreed to return with his wife, nor is it the only reason they and their three children joined the church and became actively involved. But I wonder.

Whoever you're trying to reach as a church, however you're trying to reach them, and whatever you hope God will do with their hearts and lives, know this: God will use you, the people around you, and people you haven't even met yet. God will use the tools of media to achieve God's will. And, although you may not always feel it, you have everything you need to participate with God in that. God ordains a purpose for our churches and for our ministries. God gives us values, pathways on which we can step deliberately toward that purpose. God brings people together in each church, creating a unique family or culture. God reveals his vision for our churches, leading us to change in ways that help us to serve more fully. God clarifies for us what is most important, and what is not important, and is honored by our striving to do what is important, with excellence. And God allows us to share in the joy of creation, as we pour ourselves into creating something meaningful for worship.

What happened, exactly, when my friend learned something substantial in a sermon video interview? Or when he watched that baby's sweet face dripping with baptismal waters, and heard the chorus of voices around him pledge to care for the child? What happened to him when he looked up and read those ancient and familiar words, remembering the feel of his grandmother's hand and the sound of her voice? What happened, exactly, when he prayed for the first time in twenty-five years "...Thy kingdom come, thy will be done, on earth as it is in heaven..."?

Whatever happened to him that Sunday morning might have happened if there were only bulletins and hymnals, with heads buried and voices mumbling. It might have happened even if he never saw that baby's wet shiver, or the kind eyes of that pastor. And it might have happened if everyone around him prayed that prayer while he remained silent, vaguely humiliated, because he was unable to recall the words. But I do wonder.

Who is the "tall, lanky man"—or woman, or child—for you? And what will you do now to be ready when that person walks in the front door of God's church?